The JEWISH CONNECTION to ISRAEL, the PROMISED LAND

A Brief Introduction for CHRISTIANS

RABBI EUGENE KORN, PhD

For People of All Faiths, All Backgrounds
JEWISH LIGHTS Publishing
Woodstock, Vermont

The Jewish Connection to Israel, the Promised Land:
A Brief Introduction for Christians

2008 First Printing

© 2008 by Eugene Korn

All quotations from the Hebrew Bible are taken from the *JPS Hebrew-English Tanakh* (Philadelphia: Jewish Publication Society, 1999).

Grateful acknowledgment is given for permission to use material from the following sources: The maps on pp. 30, 38, 92, 96, 124, 128, 132, 134, and 138, © 2003, are reprinted with permission from Koret Communications, Ltd., (www.koret.com). The map on p. 76 from *The Routledge Atlas of Jewish History* (ISBN 0415399653 HC, 0415399661 PB) by Martin Gilbert, © 2002, published by Routledge, reprinted with permission of Taylor & Francis Books UK. The photo on p. 102 from *The Ethiopian Jews of Israel: Personal Stories of Life in the Promised Land* by Len Lyons with photographs by Ilan Ossendryver, © 2007, published by Verve Editions/Jewish Lights Publishing and reprinted with permission from Ilan Ossendryver. The map on p. 140 from *The Missing Peace* by Dennis Ross © 1996, published by Farrar, Straus and Giroux, New York, reprinted with permission by the author and cartography by International Mapping.

Library of Congress Cataloging-in-Publication Data
Korn, Eugene, 1947–
The Jewish connection to Israel , the Promised Land : a brief introduction for Christians / Eugene Korn.
p. cm.
Includes bibliographical references.
ISBN-13: 978-1-58023-318-7 (quality pbk.)
ISBN-10: 1-58023-318-X (quality pbk.)
1. Israel. 2. Zionism. 3. Israel and the diaspora. 4. Judaism—Relations—Christianity. 5. Christianity and other religions—Judaism. I. Title.
DS126.5.K64 2008
320.54095694—dc22
2007041952

10 9 8 7 6 5 4 3 2 1
Manufactured in the United States of America
Cover Design: Melanie Robinson

For People of All Faiths, All Backgrounds
Published by Jewish Lights Publishing
A Division of LongHill Partners, Inc.
Sunset Farm Offices, Route 4, P.O. Box 237
Woodstock, VT 05091
Tel: (802) 457-4000   Fax: (802) 457-4004
www.jewishlights.com

To the millions of Jews throughout the millennia who dreamed of Zion but were never privileged to live there.

And to Christians everywhere who understand the meaning of the Holy Land to the Covenant of Abraham.

CONTENTS

LIST OF MAPS AND ILLUSTRATIONS

FROM DECLARATION OF INDEPENDENCE OF THE STATE OF ISRAEL, MAY 14, 1948

Eretz-Yisrael [the Land of Israel] was the birthplace of the Jewish people. Here their spiritual, religious, and political identity was shaped. Here they first attained to statehood, created cultural values of national and universal significance and gave to the world the eternal Book of Books.

After being forcibly exiled from their land, the people kept faith with it throughout their Dispersion and never ceased to pray and hope for their return to it and for the restoration in it of their political freedom.

Impelled by this historic and traditional attachment, Jews strove in every successive generation to re-establish themselves in their ancient homeland. In recent decades, they returned in their masses. Pioneers, *ma'pilim* [immigrants coming to *Eretz-Israel* in defiance of restrictive legislation] and defenders, they made deserts bloom, revived the Hebrew language, built villages and towns, and created a thriving community controlling its own economy and culture, loving peace but knowing how to defend itself, bringing the blessings of progress to all the country's inhabitants, and aspiring towards independent nationhood.

This right is the natural right of the Jewish people to be masters of their own fate, like all other nations, in their own sovereign State.

We appeal to the Jewish people throughout the Diaspora to rally round the Jews of *Eretz-Israel* in the tasks of immigration and building and to stand by them in the great struggle for the realization of the age-old dream—the redemption of Israel.

The Lord said to Abram,

"Go forth from your native land and from your kin and your father's house to the land that I will show you.

I will make of you a great nation, and I will bless you; I will make your name great and you shall be a blessing.

I will bless those who bless you and curse those who curse you; and all the families of the earth shall bless themselves by you."

Abram went forth as the Lord commanded him.... When they arrived in the land of Canaan, Abram passed through the land as far as the site of Shechem, at the terebinths of Moreh.

The Lord appeared to Abram and said, "I will give this land to your offspring."

—GENESIS 12:1–7, CIRCA 1700 BCE

INTRODUCTION

ISRAEL IS A WORLD STORY. It is a geographically small country
with only seven million citizens, yet it is the focus of endless
reporting in the international media. It captures the attention of
billions of people all around the world. Israel is a place of great
contradictions: a secular country but one with deep religious
meaning; a vibrant modern culture where the past beckons
every moment; a home to the Jewish people yet a democracy
for all persons; a Jewish country seeking acceptance in a region
that tolerates only Islamic authority. Perhaps Theodor Herzl
best captured the paradox at the end of the nineteenth century
in the title of his book, *Altneuland (Old-New Land)*.

The State of Israel was established in 1948, but its spiritual
and cultural roots go back more than three thousand years. The
historical experiences of the Jewish people, Jewish religion, and
Jewish culture are all deeply connected to the Land of Israel.
Since the beginning of Jewish history, the Jewish people have
had a romance with the land promised them by the Bible,[1] and
the modern country of Israel is the expression of that long historical drama. Today, Israel stands at the center of Jewish self-
perception—how most Jews see themselves individually and
collectively as a people. Israel is the stage on which Jewish life
and peoplehood is playing out most vividly in the present, and
the key to Jewish spiritual hopes for the future. In other words,
Israel is the place that most intimately connects the Jewish past,

present, and future. Grasping the reality of Israel and the Jewish people's profound attachment to the Jewish State, then, means appreciating the Bible's dream of the ideal covenantal Jewish society on the Promised Land, the Jewish people's origins on the Land, the harsh Jewish experience in exile from the Land and the Jewish people's heroic struggle for survival. Conversely, if we are to understand Jews and Judaism today, we must be aware of the hopes, dreams, and experiences that are located in contemporary Israel.

From whichever vantage point one views the Jewish State, it is clear that Israel carries two essential meanings for the Jewish people and the world. Israel is an indispensable part of the Bible's ancient challenge to Abraham's children to be a partner with God in a sacred covenant, in which the Jewish people are called to be a free self-determined people and to live as "a kingdom of priests and a holy people" (Exodus 19:6). As a sovereign Jewish homeland, Israel provides the Jewish people with a home for Jews fleeing persecution anywhere in the world. Sovereignty ensures that Jews will never again be forced to search for safety and acceptance. This is why only the reality of Israel can give real meaning to the Jewish people's hope that their future will be more secure than their past.

Unfortunately, Israel has been wracked by war for much of its short life, since it was established in 1948. Even today, too few of Israel's Arab neighbors have accepted the right of the Jewish State to exist. Transcending politics and economics, this ongoing conflict has exploited history, the Bible, theology, and national identities to produce polemical debate. As is often the case when ideology and rhetoric flourish, truth and understanding are the losers. As a result of the polemics, there is confusion regarding the political and religious realities of Israel.

Because Israel is at the center of Jewish life and identity, the Jewish State is crucial to relations between Jews and Christians. As we will see, the idea of Jews returning to their biblical homeland has long troubled Christian theologians. Some Protestant religious thinkers have difficulty connecting religion with sovereignty or national politics. Many Christians today see Israel as devoid of religious value, as a secular polity whose justification is no different from any other people's: Jews deserve a country only because all people have a universal right to self-determination. Some nontraditional Jews also understand Israel only in political terms—as a well-deserved Jewish refuge after thousands of years of persecution and exile culminating in the Holocaust. Some contemporary Christian "liberation theologians" go to an extreme and refuse to acknowledge even this. They have teamed up with extremist postnationalists to reject the idea of a Jewish homeland and to deny Israel's right to exist.

Neglecting the spiritual significance of Israel and seeing the country in exclusively political terms tends to polarize people who identify with the Jewish people against those who feel closer to the Palestinian people and the Muslim world. In the opposite direction, some evangelical Christians and Orthodox Jews view Israel in fundamentalist terms filled with messianic scenarios. So we arrive at a popular divide between some Protestant and liberal political leaders on the one hand, and Jews and conservative Christians on the other. This is still another tragic dimension of misunderstanding Israel. As Israel's Declaration of Independence makes clear, from its very birth Israel saw no need to choose between her well-being and that of her Arab neighbors. In fact the opposite is true: Most Israelis know that peace and prosperity will only be achieved when Israelis, Palestinians, Egyptians, Lebanese, Jordanians, and Syrians accept one another's right to live alongside their neighbors in safety and security.

Last, viewing Israel through political or fundamentalist lenses makes it difficult to appreciate how Jewish culture and tradition have understood the Bible, the Jewish people's attachment to the Land, and the religious significance of Jewish political independence. Seeing the developing religious dimension of Israel helps us understand modern Judaism and the unique role of the Jewish people in religious history.

Are these three dimensions of Israel—the ancient religious, the modern political, and the future spiritual—related? This book strives to show that they are, and to explain how Israel has the potential to realize the Jewish ideal of integrating the spiritual and the physical, the holy and the mundane. *The Jewish Connection to Israel, the Promised Land* attempts to describe briefly how Judaism has understood the narrative of the Bible's covenant and the role of the Jewish people in history, both of which involve the Land of Israel. As an independent Jewish homeland, Israel gives the Jewish people the first opportunity of national self-determination in almost two thousand years, to shape and live out its particular spiritual and national values. As a glimpse into the past and the present, the achievements and disappointments, joys and tragedies, dreams and realities of Israeli life today, *The Jewish Connection to Israel, the Promised Land* tries to express the personal hopes of Jews as well as the national drama of the Jewish people that unfolds every day in the Jewish State.

This book is about a people that has known too much bloodshed and persecution in its past, about its homeland in the Middle East, which is a region of constant violence, and the role this country can play in the future. I offer it in the hope that it will encourage greater knowledge of the Jewish people, and of Israel as a country whose security need not threaten its neighbors. If *The Jewish Connection to Israel, the Promised Land* contributes toward Jews', Christians', and all people's understanding one another better, it will be no small contribution to realizing the noble dream of ancient prophets and modern idealists alike, that peace and justice reign throughout the world.

PART I

THE BIBLICAL DREAM

1

LAND AND COVENANT: THE BIBLE AND THE BIRTH OF THE JEWISH PEOPLE

THE BIBLE IS THE FOUNDATION OF JEWISH CULTURE, early Jewish history, and Jewish self-understanding. In fact, most of Jewish Scripture is devoted to telling the early history of the Jewish people, the only biblical people that has survived until today. The Bible describes the birth of the Jewish people— sometime during the Bronze Age around 1700 BCE[1]—in God's challenges and promises to Abraham, the father of the Jewish people. At the genesis of Jewish identity, God instructs the patriarch Abraham (then called Abram) to leave his native society of Mesopotamia in the region of the Tigris and Euphrates rivers, travel westward, and begin a new people and a new culture in the Land of Canaan on the Mediterranean Sea:

> The Lord said to Abram, "Go out of your native land and from your father's house to the land that I will show you. I will make of you a great nation and I will bless you; I will make your name great, and you shall be a blessing. I will bless those who bless you and curse those you curse you; And all the families of the earth shall bless themselves by you.... And the Lord appeared to Abram and said, "*I will assign this land to your offspring* [emphasis mine]." (Genesis 12:1–3, 7)

Shortly thereafter, the Bible emphasizes that Abram and his people will inherit the land forever by virtue of the covenant:

> The Lord said to Abram … "Raise your eyes and look out from where you are, to the north and south, to the east and west, for I give all the land that you see to you and your offspring forever…. [Get] up, walk about the land, through its length and its breadth, for I give it to you." (Genesis 13:14–17)

Throughout Jewish history, religious and secular Jews alike have understood this account of Abraham's journey as the beginning of their people's story. The land to which Abram migrated later took the name *Eretz Yisrael* (the Land of Israel), after Abraham's descendents, the Israelite people. The Bible describes God's promise to Abraham as the beginning of a special covenantal relationship between God and the Jewish people. A covenant is a sacred contract, and as in every contract, each party acquires benefits in return for assuming responsibilities. For Abraham, the benefits of the covenant are clear: blessing, nationhood, and title to the Land. But Genesis 12 does not indicate any covenantal obligations or responsibilities that Abraham or his children must bear.

According to the covenant, Abraham and his descendants—the Jewish people—are destined to play a role in universal human history: "You shall be a blessing…. All the families of the earth shall bless themselves by you" (Genesis 12:2–3). The covenant demands that the Jewish people cannot be a parochial or ghetto people, or an insignificant footnote to the larger drama of humanity. God's covenantal people must be a central actor in universal history. The Book of Genesis repeats this universal dimension of the covenant five times, twice more when God reestablishes the covenant with Abraham (18:18 and 22:17–22), when the covenant is passed to

Abraham's son, Isaac, (26:4), and in turn when it is bequeathed to Isaac's son, Jacob (28:13–14). It seems clear that the Bible considers this universal role an essential part of Jewish covenantal destiny and mission. One of the Bible's paradoxes is that the covenant asks a particular people in a particular place to have a universal mission and impact on human history.

It is also important that immediately after first hearing of the covenant, the Bible tells us that Abraham built an altar and called the name of God (Genesis 12:7–9). The Bible describes the covenant in Chapter 13, when Abraham again responds by calling the name of God. In other words, he makes the presence of God known to the people around him, "bearing witness" to the presence and majesty of God in the world. The phrase sounds Christian, but the idea of "witness" is authentic to Jewish Scripture and Judaism. Christianity borrowed this religious idea from its Jewish roots and applied it in different ways. A traditional rabbinic interpretation states that "before Abraham, God was called 'God of the heavens'; after Abraham, people called Him 'God of the heavens and the earth.'"[2] In other words, through the covenant, God challenged Abraham to teach the world that God dwells on earth—not just in heaven—and is a partner in human affairs.

LAND AS THE PLACE OF THE COVENANT

Jews know Jewish Scripture as *Torah*, which is Hebrew for "teaching."[3] (Christians have traditionally referred to the Hebrew Bible as the Old Testament, but many Christian scholars now more properly refer to it as Hebrew Scriptures or Shared Scriptures.) Almost every time the Torah refers to the covenant, the gift of the Land is mentioned. This is true throughout Genesis: God tells Abraham his descendants will be strangers in a foreign land but will return home to reclaim the Land

(15:13–18); when God tells Isaac that he will inherit his father's divine legacy but that he may not leave the Land (Genesis 26:1–5); God informs Jacob, Isaac's son, that he will bear the covenant of Abraham (Genesis 28:13–15); Jacob tells his son, Joseph the viceroy of Egypt, that God will bring him back to the land of his fathers to continue the covenant (Genesis 48:21).

One of the central motifs of the Book of Exodus is the liberation from Egyptian slavery so that Jews may live free in the land of their ancestors. This is announced early in Exodus. Later, after the famous incident of worshiping the golden calf, the Bible also connects the Land to the reassertion of the covenant. Moses convinces God not to forsake the Jewish people and to hold fast to the divine covenant with them, pleading:

> Turn from Your blazing anger and renounce the plan to punish Your people. Remember Your servants, Abraham, Isaac and Israel, how You swore to them by Your Self and said to them: I will make your offspring as numerous as the stars of heaven, and *I will give your offspring this whole land of which I spoke to possess forever* [emphasis mine]. (Exodus 32:12–13)

God accepts Moses' plea and reasserts the covenant as follows:

> Set out from here, you and the people that you have brought up from the land of Egypt *to the land of which I swore to Abraham, Isaac and Jacob, saying, "To your offspring will I give it…. I hereby make a covenant* [italics mine]. Before all your people I will work such wonders as have not been wrought on earth…. Mark well what I command you this day. I will drive out before you the Amorites, the Canaanites, the Hittites, the Perizzites, the Hivites, and the Jebusites. (33:1; 34:10–12)

Leviticus, Numbers, and Deuteronomy all emphasize the same connection between Jewish destiny, sacred covenant, and the Land. Both Numbers and Deuteronomy are a record of the Jewish people's travels in preparation for the Israelites' entering the Land of Canaan, where they can fulfill their national and religious missions. Deuteronomy even devotes considerable detail to how the Jewish people should divide the Land among the twelve tribes of Israel and how plots of land must be inherited from generation to generation. Entering the Promised Land remained Moses' most profound wish all his life:

> I pleaded with the Lord at that time, saying, "O Lord God, You who let Your servant see the first works of Your greatness and Your mighty hand. You whose powerful deeds no god in heaven or on earth can equal. Let me, I pray, cross over and see the good land on the other side of the Jordan." (Deuteronomy 3:23–25)

According to the narrative in the Bible, God rejected Moses' poignant plea and refused him entry into Canaan. Moses carried his dream of the Land with him until his death, and so in his last words, Moses reminds his people of God's covenant and promise of the Land:

> I am now one hundred and twenty years old, I can no longer be active.... Then Moses called Joshua and said to him in the sight of all Israel: "Be strong and resolute, for it is you who shall go with this people into the Land that the Lord swore to their fathers to give them." ... That day Moses wrote down this poem and taught it to the Israelites. And He charged Joshua son of Nun: "Be strong and resolute: for you shall bring the Israelites into the

Land that I promised them on oath, and I will be with you. (Deuteronomy 31:2, 7–8, 22–23)

The biblical story from Abraham to Moses is how Jews—both religious and secular—understand their national, cultural, and religious origins. This narrative has formed the foundation of Jewish historical and cultural memory, and for how Jews understand themselves as a nation. The Bible does not explain why this specific geographic locale should be necessary to the sacred mission commanded by the God of the heavens, earth, and all humanity, but it is clear that for the Bible, the Land is essential to the divine biblical mission.

THE UNIQUENESS OF THE LAND

The Bible makes one more critical point about the Land of Canaan. That land is unique and was chosen for a specific reason. It is unlike any other land, and the Bible emphasizes that no other homeland would be conducive to the Jewish people fulfilling their sacred covenant. While the Bible describes the Land of Israel as "a land of milk and honey" (Deuteronomy 31:20) and "a good land, a land with streams and springs and fountains issuing from plain and hill; a land of wheat and barley, of vines, figs, and pomegranates; a land of olive trees and honey" (Deuteronomy 8:7–8), Scripture also points out on numerous occasions that this land forces its inhabitants to recognize God by increasing the Jewish people's dependency on God and on fulfilling the covenant:

The Land that you are about to enter and possess is not like the land of Egypt from which you have come. There the grain you sowed had to be watered by your own labors, like a vegetable garden; but the Land you are about to cross into and possess, a land of hills and valleys, soaks up its water from the rains of the heavens. It is a Land which the Lord your God looks after, on which the Lord your God always keeps His eye, from year's beginning to year's end. If, then, you obey the commandments that I enjoin you this day, loving the Lord your God and serving him with all your heart and soul, I will grant the rain for your land in season. (Deuteronomy 11:10–13)

Unlike Egypt, where life was organized around the constant ebb and flow of the mighty Nile River, the Land of Canaan has no great rivers and few natural water sources. Living on this land, then, forces its inhabitants to depend on rain from the heavens. If God is gracious and offers rain generously, life prospers; when there is little or no rain, nature and human life wither. So life on the Land should produce a natural God-consciousness and remind the Jewish people of their obligations under the covenant.

From its initial appearance in Genesis through to its final appearance in Deuteronomy, the covenant is consistently explained in connection with the Land of Israel. For the Bible, as well as Judaism and Jewish culture that developed out of the Jewish understanding of the biblical story, life on the Land is necessary to God's covenant and for the Jewish people to play its role in human history.

COVENANTAL OBLIGATIONS

The terms of the covenant unfold gradually in the Bible. It is only in Genesis 18 that we see the first statement of Abraham's obligations, of how Abraham and his descendants are obligated to live in order to bring God's name into the world. There, for some reason, God decides to engage Abraham in his decision before destroying the cities of Sodom and Gomorrah:

> Shall I hide from Abraham what I am about to do, since Abraham is to become a great and populous nation and all the nations of the earth are to bless themselves by him? For I have singled him out, that he may instruct his children and his posterity to keep the way of the Lord, by doing what is just and right, in order that the Lord may bring about for Abraham what He has promised him. (Genesis 18:17–19)

Destined to be God's covenantal partner, Abraham stands obligated to keep the way of the Lord, which is "to do what is just (*mishpat*) and right (*tzedakah*)." In the Bible, *tzedakah* indicates righteous behavior through charity and compassion. *Mishpat* is justice based on faithfulness to law and fair legal standards.[4] Thus the covenant calls upon Abraham and his descendants to create a new society based on compassion and justice, and to be living models who teach these ideals to humanity. Creating a society around those values, and acting in ways for all to see, mercy and justice are the primary ways that the Jewish people are asked to live the covenant and show their commitment to God.

This explains why God informs Abraham about the planned divine destruction of the two wicked cities: Not distinguishing between the innocent and the guilty is the clearest violation of justice. By announcing the divine plan, God tested Abraham to determine if he is sufficiently committed to fight the injustice of punishing the innocent persons of the cities. If Abraham were not so committed, I suspect he would have been disqualified as the father of the covenantal people.

Abraham passed the test by protesting God's plan and challenging God with an audacious moral argument: "Far be it from You … to bring death upon the innocent as well as the guilty…. Shall not the Judge of all the earth deal justly?" (Genesis 18:25). Abraham's commitment to justice distinguishes him from Noah, who did not express any concern to God about whether innocent people would perish in the flood. Perhaps this lack of concern explains why Noah did not become the father of the covenantal people committed to justice, and why Jewish tradition was skeptical about the depth of Noah's righteousness.

2

NATIONAL LIFE, HOLINESS, AND POLITICS: JEWISH DESTINY AND THE COVENANTAL DREAM

WHY THE LAND OF ISRAEL?

THE BIBLE DOES NOT TELL US WHY THE LAND IS ESSENTIAL, but it is clear from the numerous biblical passages cited in the previous chapter that the Bible considers the Land to be a necessary part of the covenant. And this is perplexing: If Abraham and his people contract a sacred covenant with the Creator of the entire universe, with God Who is incorporeal and therefore not limited to any specific location, and if Abraham's mission is to teach that this omnipresent God is available to all the families of the earth in all places, then a particular geographic location appears unnecessary. Why could Abraham not fulfill this divine mission in Ur of Mesopotamia or in Haran—or why, thousands of years later, cannot the Jewish people carry out this mission in New York, Paris, or Cairo?

When the early Christians broke with Judaism and the Jewish people to become "the New Israel," it asked this question. Christianity also accepted the importance of the divine biblical covenant, but understood the message of early Christianity to transfer the blessings and obligations of the covenant from the

Jewish people to those accepting Christianity. In other words, Christianity had superseded Judaism, and Christians had replaced Jews as God's partner in the biblical covenant. This became known as the doctrine of supersessionism, and one of the most remarkable positive religious developments in the last fifty years is that all major church denominations have come to accept that God's covenant with Israel is irrevocable and that Judaism as a covenant between God and the Jewish people is still a living valid religion.[1] Both Judaism and Christianity coexist as living religions. (As we will see, this turn in Christian thinking implies that Christians should think anew about the importance of the Land and Jewish nationhood for Christianity. If the Jewish covenant with God is still valid, then so is the religious and spiritual importance—even for Christianity—of the land of the biblical covenant and Jewish national life on the Land.)

Nevertheless, the early church "universalized" the particular covenant with the Jewish people and extended it to all Christian believers everywhere. When this happened, the necessity of living in a specific local geography was both physically impossible and logically unnecessary. So from the time of the church fathers Tertullian and Origen in the early third century, Christian theology felt the need to universalize the place of the covenant by interpreting references to the Land of Israel metaphorically. Ultimately the role of the Land in the covenant was replaced by the body of Christ.[2] Of course, even Christianity could not completely eliminate its connection to the Land of Israel, and still has enormous religious, emotional, and historical attachment to Jerusalem, Bethlehem, Nazareth, and the Galilee region of Israel. Throughout the ages up to today, Christians lived in these locations, and Christian pilgrims continued to visit their holy sites. In the Middle Ages, Christian armies marched from Europe to Palestine in an attempt to conquer Jerusalem from Muslim forces. So despite its "spiritualization" of holiness, Christianity understood that land, place, and some physical reality are necessary for holiness to be real and compelling.

Judaism stayed close to the biblical expression of the covenant, which undergoes a fundamental change between Genesis and Exodus. The first eleven chapters of Genesis tell a cosmic story about the creation of the universe and the development of humanity. Beginning with chapter 12, Genesis becomes the family story of Abraham through Joseph and his siblings, Abraham's great-grandsons. However, in the Book of Exodus, the Abrahamic clan evolves into a nation, and the covenant changes from a sacred contract with a small family to one with a people. It becomes a *national* covenant with the Jewish people as a collective.

This occurs most explicitly in the Bible in the dramatic experience of revelation, when the Jewish people stands at Sinai immediately before receiving the Ten Commandments:

> And Moses went up to God. The Lord called to him from the top of the mountain, saying: "Thus shall you say to the house of Jacob and declare to the children of Israel: 'You have seen what I did to the Egyptians, how I bore you on eagles' wings and brought you to Me. Now then, if you will obey Me faithfully and keep My covenant, you shall be My treasured possession from all the peoples. Indeed, all the earth is Mine, but you shall be to Me a kingdom of priests and a holy nation.'" (Exodus 19:3–6)

This is the moment of election, and the statement of the covenant is with *the Jews as a people, rather than with individuals*. Judaism is the story of a particular nation and the role the Jewish people must play in sacred human history. In Exodus, the *nation* now assumes the same divine mission that Abraham had: God calls the Jewish people as a collective to be witnesses to the presence of God on earth by living a life of holiness. Election is not superiority, but responsibility, which carries with it both blessing and curse. The Bible demands that Jews not be a normal people like all others, but an eternal people with a unique history. As a divine contract, the Bible is clear that covenantal relationship between the Jewish people and God is eternal and cannot be revoked.[3] But the same covenant that promises the reward of the Land and blessing when the Jewish people fulfill its covenantal responsibilities also promises harsh punishments of exile from the Land when the Jewish people as a people violates God's covenant. In the words of Leviticus, when Jews living on the Land adopt idolatrous practices and do not keep God's commandments, "the Land will vomit you out" (18:24–27). Thus biblical Jewish history is a sacred drama of reward and punishment, of life on the Land and exile from it.[4] Though Israel may disobey, the covenantal relationship between God and the people of Israel is eternal and will never be broken.

HOLINESS AND THE COVENANT

The quest for holiness is not unique to the Bible's covenant or the Jewish people. Holiness is a fundamental goal of every religious person who seeks transcendent meaning. Thus every spiritual tradition has a conception of holiness and tries to realize it in different ways. What does the biblical challenge for the Jewish people to be "a kingdom of priests and a holy nation" mean? The Torah spells out its particular idea of holiness and its program for holy living most explicitly in the Book of Leviticus, where God formally commands the Jewish people with the obligation to lead a holy life:

> The Lord spoke to Moses saying, "Speak to the whole Israelite community and say to them, 'You shall be holy, for I, the Lord your God, am holy.'" (Leviticus 19:1–2)

The original Hebrew text of this passage is important. The imperative to be holy appears in the plural form (*Kedoshim tehiyu* in Hebrew) to emphasize that the commandment is addressed to corporate Israel, not separately to each individual Jew. Israel is commanded to achieve national holiness; the Jewish people *as a people* are charged to mirror God through the holy life. Jewish corporate life is the sine qua non of the biblical covenantal dream. This is a major distinction between Jewish and Christian theologies. Jews do not talk of individual salvation. When we read Hebrew Scripture closely, we do not find the promise of individual salvation. There is the history and future of a people, national return and redemption in naturalistic terms; the sacred covenant is played out on a collective level within empirical history.

The biblical dream is for the people of Israel to demonstrate holiness primarily through public actions and behavior rather than through private creed.

> When you reap the harvest of your land ... you shall leave them [the crops of the corners of the field] for the poor and the stranger....
>
> You shall not steal; you shall not deal deceitfully or falsely with one another....
>
> You shall not defraud your fellow. You shall not commit robbery. The wages of a laborer shall not remain with you until morning.
>
> You shall not insult the deaf, or place a stumbling block before the blind....
>
> You shall not render an unfair decision; do not favor the poor or show deference to the rich; judge your kinsman fairly. Do not deal basely with your countrymen. Do not profit by the blood of your fellow....

> You shall not hate your kinsfolk in your heart. Reprove
> your kinsmen but incur no guilt because of him. You shall
> not take vengeance or bear a grudge against your country-
> men. Love your fellow as yourself. (Leviticus 19:9–18)

In this text, all expressions of holiness are social. Life and human relationships are the raw materials that must be shaped according to the Bible's spiritual values. Holiness, *Kedushah*, is achieved by sacred action, by creating relationships of responsibility and caring for one another—and in the process forming a people who brings God's values to earth. The Bible is concerned with the values, norms, and standards of interpersonal behavior that exist in the community; holiness is measured by the quality of interpersonal actions. The above verses give examples from a wide variety of social contexts about how to behave in accordance with a holy life. Great Rabbis like Akiva of Talmudic times and Nachmanides during the Middle Ages understood the particular examples of those verses to be summed up by the concluding general commandment of Leviticus, verse 18: "Love your fellow as yourself."

What kind of society is a holy society? In the biblical covenantal vision, it is one where the disparity between the rich and poor is minimized by laws of charity and welfare. It is a society where each person regards his or her neighbor as having intrinsic sanctity because he or she is created in God's holy image and not as a finite object to be used. It is a society where the law upholds the dignity of all and protects the interests of the vulnerable, and where people learn to feel a deep identification and responsibility for one another through communal and social practices. To be a holy people means to construct a society in which the behavioral norms of Leviticus 19 form the primary national ethos and the roots of the society's structure.

The Bible articulates another value at the end of Leviticus, chapter 19:33:

> If a stranger lives with you in the Land, do not oppress him. He shall be like a native. You shall love the stranger as yourself, for you were strangers in Egypt.

This is no insignificant part of the covenant, or some isolated passage that clashes with the main thrust of the Bible's message. This one commandment appears in various forms no less than thirty-six times: Be compassionate and resist oppressing the vulnerable—the stranger, the widow, the orphan, and the poor. The ideal holy society is not a monolithically Jewish community, but a society where gentiles are welcomed, where justice is present for all, where compassion for the stranger flows freely, and where all respect and protect the dignity of the disadvantaged among them.

HOLINESS IN THE PHYSICAL WORLD

In fact, the role of the Land in the covenant is a central part of a much broader Jewish theology that unites the sweep of Jewish sacred history with the ideal of everyday sacred Jewish living. I would encapsulate it as follows: For Judaism, redemption is a historical, not a metaphysical, category. In other words, the process and ideal of salvation take place within empirical history and physical experience. The human mission of the divine covenant is for the Jewish people to influence human history so that it marches toward a state of affairs where righteousness and justice prevail, and where human beings are aware of the authority and presence of God on earth. The fulfillment of the covenant is the dream of the ideal society in the messianic age. The idea of the messianic age is the birth of a new ideal unknown in the rest of the ancient and classical word: the idea of historical progress. Pagans understood history to be random, while Plato and Aristotle understood history to be cyclical with no hope of overcoming poverty, violence, or injustice.[5] The biblical ideal is achieved not primarily by grace, but through human striving, teaching, and, above all, through human moral action. In this way, humans and God are partners in perfecting the world and completing the cosmic creation that God began.

The Bible understands that history is influenced more by societies and cultures than by isolated individuals, so it calls on a particular people, the Jewish people, to be a "kingdom of priests," or, in Isaiah's terminology, "a light unto the nations" (Isaiah 42:6, 49:6). It asks the Jews to be an exemplary people that teaches these values and is a model to others for holy living. (In biblical Judaism, priests are primarily leaders and teachers, not intermediaries.) The Jewish people's task is to bring the Infinite into history and finite human experience and thereby redeem human life. Judaism is therefore not so much a religion of belief as it is a structured lifestyle of deeds on earth. The covenantal commandments constitute the guidelines for translating this lofty vision into the particular actions of everyday life. This is the essence of biblical history and the Jewish covenantal drama, and, as the Talmud says, "all the rest is commentary" (*Shabbat* 31a).

If this is correct, then for Jews, "incarnation" does not refer to God but to the holiness of God's spirit that people can feel unmistakably in the course of their finite and earthly experiences. Through holy living, people infuse the physical world— the carnal world—with a spiritual and infinite dimension. Judaism rejected the value of escaping from the physical world. For Plato, the ideal was for the soul to break out of "the prison-house" of the body or the physical world. Augustine also taught that human experience was a conflicting dualism between the flesh and the spirit that could not be combined. Some philosophers gave up on any real value existing in the world. (They are known as nihilists—people who believe in nothing.) They had an attitude of *contemptus mundi*—contempt for life and rejection of the world. By contrast, Judaism teaches that life attains value by endowing it with holiness. Physical experience becomes holy when people combine it with a spiritual dimension. It is no accident that the sign of the Jewish covenant is circumcision, a mark of spiritual commitment literally cut into the physical body, and that the requirement of circumcision became one of the primary dividing points between traditional Judaism and early Christianity. For Judaism, the covenant demands the combination of the spiritual with the material. Holiness is the product of a dialectical interaction of the body and the spirit, and cannot exist without both.

Of course, in the Bible and Jewish religious life, holiness is achieved by more than ethical social relations. The demand to be a holy people—and therefore the scope of Judaism as a religion—applies to all human strivings, to all areas of life: agriculture, economics, justice, charity, truth-telling, business, ritual, and politics. Commandments for holy action appear also in Leviticus 18 and 20 relating to sexuality,[6] in Leviticus 20 relating to sacrifices and eating meat,[7] in Leviticus 23 celebrating sacred times of the calendar, such as the Sabbath and the holidays,[8] and in Leviticus 21 relating to avoiding contact with death.[9] Like land and politics, all of these refer to arenas of human physical experience. Biblical and rabbinic doctrine deem every major arena of human endeavor as sanctified. There is no permanently secular domain. Everything can be redeemed.

HOLINESS AND LAND

We have seen that the biblical covenant for Jews to be a holy people focuses on the Jewish people as a collective and on the performance of deeds that bring holiness into human experience in all areas of social, political, personal, and physical life. But for the people of Israel to be the instrument of realizing God's covenant in empirical history, there must be a place where that sacred history can be freely played out. The Jewish people must live in a place where *as a people* it is free to pursue its unique ideals and structure its society according to those values. It must be in a place where it can be in control of the major areas of its life so it can determine its character as a national group and command its own destiny. Cultural and moral independence is indispensable to the covenantal dream and the life of the covenantal people.

The Bible understood what human history has taught all nations: Freedom for a people can only occur when that nation has sovereignty in its own land. Land and sovereignty are necessary conditions for Jewish self-determination in both the political and spiritual sense. Only when these are assured can the Jewish people be free to live out its dream and accept responsibility for its own laws, values, and standards. If holiness were confined to the private sphere, to belief, or to one small corner of public life, then the covenant could be realized independent of political and national freedom. But according to the Bible, the covenant and holy living apply to all actions, and hence national independence is a necessity. Land and sovereignty are historical necessities, not intrinsic spiritual ideals. This is the reason why, given the Bible's idea of holiness within society, the Land of Israel is a prime necessity for Israel to fulfill its national and spiritual mission of bringing the message of God and blessing to humanity.

The Land itself, however, does not contain the sacred, nor does sovereignty guarantee holiness. It merely presents *the possibility* of achieving a holy society and people. Realizing that possibility is the biblical challenge of the individual spiritual life and sacred human history. The biblical concept of holiness that fuses the physical and the spiritual requires a careful balance that is difficult to achieve. Throughout history, Jews have at times departed from the biblical ideal of holiness and substituted alternative spiritual ideas that abandoned this delicate equilibrium. During the Second Temple period and the time of Jesus, the Essenes celebrated religious purity, which meant asceticism and abandonment of society, and today there are sectarian ultra-Orthodox Jews who are quietists that reject any Jewish place in naturalistic history. Yet ultimately, both Jewish tradition and the majority of the Jewish people have rejected the impulse to withdraw from society and political history as practiced by these marginal groups. Jewish life and law consider Jews who practice isolation or asceticism as sinners who betray their covenantal responsibility. Avoiding the problematics of politics, war, wealth, biology, and human sexuality does not eradicate evil from God's world or from human experience. On the contrary, evil becomes a greater reality in history, because withdrawal abandons creation to the unredeemed forces of materialism and hedonism. Yet if political, biological, economic, and social life are to be redeemed by a people under the ideals of the covenant, that people must have the power to control how it lives in these areas of experience. This is only possible in a specific society, in a specific place, and on a specific land.

3

JEWISH SOVEREIGNTY IN THE ANCIENT WORLD

JUDGES, KINGS, AND THE FIRST COMMONWEALTH

AFTER MOSES' DEATH, Jews entered Canaan as a people divided into twelve tribes under Joshua's leadership in approximately 1230 BCE. This was the beginning of independent Jewish national life, which spanned the rule of judges, kings, prophets, and two commonwealths. During this period Canaan became known as Israel and Judea, after its Jewish inhabitants. Except for some seventy years, Jewish sovereignty was continuous until 67 CE, when the Romans destroyed the Jewish capital of Jerusalem and its national site, the Second Temple (and later expelled Jews from the country in 135 CE after the unsuccessful Jewish revolt led by Bar Kochba against Roman rule).[1] This period of sovereign Jewish life was no idyllic experience, but one of difficult political evolution, confrontations with different cultures, economic struggle, and internal divisions.

Since Israel is located at the crossroads of Africa, Europe, and Asia, Jews living there from ancient times until today have been caught in the conflicts between the mighty civilizations of the East and the West. In the ancient era, this meant that the Israelites had to battle the Canaanites, Philistines, Assyrians, Babylonians, Greeks, and Romans, among others, for geographic and political control of the Land. (Modern-day visitors

to Israel see archaeological remains of all these civilizations.)
Of all these ancient peoples, only the Jewish people have survived. Upon entering the Land, the Jewish people left behind
the life of desert wandering and biblical miracles to build a
society around the forces of natural, political, economic, and
cultural change. This ancient experience permanently influenced Jewish culture, religion, memory, and love of place that
Jews carry with them up to this day.

The Book of Joshua and historical evidence indicate that
the Jewish or Israelite people entered Canaan as an organized
union of twelve tribes that were descended from the sons of
the biblical Jacob. During the conquest, the tribes developed
considerable unity that reflected a common national goal. The
disunited Canaanite inhabitants were unable to withstand the
onslaught of the Israelite tribes, and under Joshua's leadership,
the Israelites succeeded in taking possession of the hill country
running from north to south along the central mountain
region. (Many contemporary cities like Nablus, Hebron, and
Bethlehem are in these very locations.) The Philistines
remained in the lower coastal plain.

The Israelites tribes occupied an ethnically homogeneous
area. A few Canaanite enclaves remained, but they exercised
almost no influence on the cultural and social reality of Jewish
life of that time.[2] The Israelites never merged with the surrounding pagan peoples or their idolatrous religions. This ethnic and religious distinctiveness became the wellspring of an
original national Israelite culture in which belief in one God
was central. The Land of Canaan provided the geographical setting for the development of Jewish monotheistic civilization.[3]

The Israelite political organization during this period
reflects this distinctive Jewish life and culture. The surrounding
Canaanite politics was organized by cities and states that were
ruled by one king, but the Jews formed a confederation with

no central government or national ruler. They considered themselves bound in responsibility to each other by a covenant and common God. The national covenant was embodied in a shrine, the Ark of the Covenant, which ultimately was placed in the small city of Shiloh. Ordinarily, the tribes governed themselves independently or in a loose alliance. From time to time charismatic individuals emerged to lead groups of the twelve tribes. These are the famous "judges" of the Bible, among them Deborah, Gideon, and Samson, and the early prophets like Samuel. The Israelite tribes gradually became an agricultural people that lived off the Land, while establishing towns and clearing forests and wildernesses.

THE KINGS OF ISRAEL

For close to two hundred years (1230–1050 BCE) this confederation resisted centralized rule, but the nearby Philistines became an aggressive military power that conquered Shiloh, seized the Ark, and began to occupy much of the Land. The Israelites responded by opting for a king that could coordinate the fight against the Philistines. Saul was elected the first king of Israel, but he proved unable to defeat the Philistine armies. His successor was King David, who reigned from 1000 BCE to 960 BCE and succeeded in defeating the Philistines. David also conquered a Jebusite enclave in the middle of the country and named it Jerusalem, which means "city of peace" in Hebrew. He recaptured the Ark and brought it to Jerusalem, making the city the capital of the First Jewish Commonwealth, the center of Jewish national life and the heart of the Jewish religion. Since the time of David, Jerusalem has been the symbol of Jewish dreams and moral ideals, and the place from which Jews believe that redemption and knowledge of God will emanate. Its alternate name is Zion, and the prophet Isaiah proclaimed, "From Zion shall come Torah and the Word of God from Jerusalem" (Isaiah 2:3).

Although Jerusalem was occupied many times by different cultures, no other people in history made Jerusalem their spiritual and political capital. As a ruler, warrior, musician, poet, and religious leader, King David became the most beloved figure in Jewish history. The belief in Israel's ultimate redemption was eventually bound up with David and his dynasty, and the last redeemer, the Messiah, will be a descendant of David. (This is why the New Testament traces Jesus' lineage to King David.) Even today, Jews visit David's grave in Jerusalem, walk in the paths of the original Jerusalem that he established (known as the City of David), read his Psalms, and research the history of his rule.

David's monarchy consisted of two distinct geographical regions: the southern area of Judea, named after the tribe of Judah, and the area of the northern tribes, known collectively as Israel. David was succeeded by his son Solomon, who reigned in Jerusalem from 961 BCE to 922 BCE and built the First Temple there. Jews made pilgrimages from all parts of the land to Jerusalem to participate in the Temple services during the three annual pilgrimage festivals of Passover (*Pesach*), Weeks (*Shavuot*), and Tabernacles (*Sukkot*). The Temple was the location of religious sacrifices, priestly ceremonies, and holiday convocations. The highest court of the land, called the Sanhedrin, met on its outskirts. The Temple therefore became the center of religious life for the entire commonwealth, as well as the geographical symbol of Jewish national identity. Solomon's Temple became famous in the ancient world for its magnificent size and architectural grandeur, while the city of Jerusalem became the focus of Jewish dreams for national well-being, as the label "City of Peace" implies.

During the eighty years of David's and Solomon's rule, the Jewish nation achieved prosperity and created a rich literary culture that produced many of the books of the Bible that chronicled Joshua's entry into the Land and the period of the judges and the monarchy. Those two generations of life in Judea and Israel also transformed the Jewish nation from a loose confederation of farmers and shepherds to a more stratified and economically sophisticated national culture.

Solomon expanded the Israelite kingdom beyond its biblical borders, but during the reign of his son, Rehoboam, the southern region of Judah and the northern region of Israel broke their union. The northern region survived several short-lived dynasties until it was conquered and destroyed by the Assyrian Empire in 721 BCE. The Assyrians deported many of the ten tribes residing in Israel to upper Mesopotamia and replaced them with Syrians and Babylonians, whom the Assyrians also vanquished. The exiled tribes never reentered Jewish history or the Land of Israel, and they became known as "the ten lost tribes of Israel."

The southern kingdom of Judah, which consisted of the tribes of Judah and Benjamin and included Jerusalem, was left intact but subordinate to the Assyrians. Eventually the Assyrian Empire collapsed under the advance of the Babylonians at the end of the seventh century BCE. At that time, Judea was caught in the war between the Babylonian Empire to the east and the Egyptian Empire to the south. During this war, the Babylonians destroyed Judea in 602 BCE. When the Jews tried to revolt under their puppet king, Zedekiah, the army of the Babylonian king, Nebuchadnezzar, broke through the walls of Jerusalem in 587 BCE and burned the city to the ground.

The First Commonwealth and Jewish national independence had lasted more than four hundred years, from 1020 BCE to 587 BCE. When Nebuchadnezzar exiled the Jews of Judea,

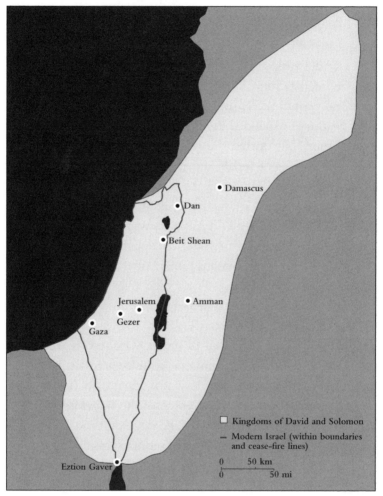

Damascus

Dan

Beit Shean

Jerusalem
Gezer

Amman

Gaza

☐ Kingdoms of David and Solomon
— Modern Israel (within boundaries
and cease-fire lines)

0   50 km
0   50 mi

Eztion Gaver

The Kingdoms of David and Solomon: 1077 - 997 BCE

they took the memory of the kingdom with them and nourished themselves on the dream of returning to Zion and restoring Jewish independence in their homeland. Their longing has been immortalized in this popular passage from the Book of Psalms:

> By the rivers of Babylon, there we sat and wept as we thought of Zion.…
>> How can we sing a song of the Lord on alien soil?
> (Psalm 137:1, 4)

The memory and longing for home was not confined to the ancient Jews of Babylon. Even today, Jews recite this passage from Psalms before they say grace after meals and during traditional wedding ceremonies.

THE PROPHETS OF ISRAEL

Biblical prophecy—the inspiring wisdom of Amos, Isaiah, Jeremiah, and others—was another defining religious and cultural development that emerged from Judea and Israel during this period. The prophets rose to prominence between 750 BCE and 400 BCE, when the Jewish nation experienced drought, famine, destruction, captivity, and, most important, the social disintegration caused by the more affluent Jews' lack of concern for their poor, orphaned, and widowed brothers and sisters. Indeed, the call of the biblical prophets was for Israel to return to the values of the God's covenant as expressed in Leviticus. In Isaiah's imagery, their indignation flowed like a mighty stream, and became the rock of Israelite religion during this time. The teachings of these prophets helped shape the values of Judeo-Christian culture throughout history.

The Bible from Genesis through Deuteronomy contains a mixture of moral, ritual, and civil law, but the prophets emphasized morality and the values of compassion, charity, honesty, and justice. They raised morality to the level of an absolute value because they regarded ethics as divine. In the eyes of the prophets, ethical values were the essence of God's personality and how God relates to all creatures. During this period, Jews living in Judea further distanced themselves from paganism, whose gods were cruel and arbitrary and abused human beings. This prophetic understanding of God became the basis for much of the later Judeo-Christian views on God, the world, history, and human life.

The revolutionary idea of the prophets was that history is decided by moral behavior in society. Because the Jews were free and independent, they were held responsible for both the moral virtues and the ills of their society. Religious sins almost always translated into moral failing. Amos repeatedly emphasizes this:

> They [the rich] recline by every altar
> On garments taken in pledge,
> And drink in the house of their God
> Wine bought with fines they imposed. (Amos 2:8)

Isaiah regarded Israel's subordination to Assyria as chastisement for sin and incentive for Israel to repent. Through repentance and righteousness, Israel could remake humanity and help it progress toward the end of history, the messianic era. Isaiah's vision was one of universal harmony and brotherhood:

> And they shall beat their swords into plowshares
> And their spears into pruning hooks:
> Nation shall not take up sword against nation;
> They shall never again know war. (Isaiah 2:2–4)

The wolf shall dwell with the lamb,
The leopard lie down with the kid;
the calf, the beast of prey, and the fatling shall feed together,
With a little boy to herd them....
For the land shall be filled with devotion to the Lord
As water covers the sea. (Isaiah 11:6, 9)

The prophet Jeremiah foresaw the destruction of Jerusalem and the exile of the Jewish people, and attributed it to moral corruption in Jewish society. But he too had a universal vision and understood that Jewish moral return to covenantal values and physical return to the Land of Israel was always possible. Israel was God's eternal people, and God's covenant was irrevocable. The marriage between God and Israel was never-ending. Speaking in God's name, he announced:

I will make an everlasting covenant with them that I will not turn away from them and that I will treat them graciously; and I will put in their hearts reverence for Me, so that they do not turn away from Me. (Jeremiah 32:40)

Another prophet, Hosea, proclaimed the same eternal covenantal marriage between God and the Jewish people:

I will espouse you forever.
I will espouse you with righteousness and justice,
And with goodness and mercy,
And I will espouse you with faithfulness. (Hosea 2:21–22)

According to the prophets' dream, all human society will move toward the triumph of justice and peace through the efforts of human beings taking responsibility for themselves and for history. Paradoxically, in all the universal prophetic dreams, the

Jewish people have returned to their particular place—to their homeland and specifically to Jerusalem—from which God's knowledge will radiate to all peoples. It is no accident that the prophetic dreams were nurtured and expressed while Jews were living in Judea and Israel, developing their own values and culture. Only a free people can be fully responsible for its society and others. Only in their own land can Jews as a people fully realize the covenantal dream. It is doubtful that the prophets could have emerged in exile. In fact, it is a strong Jewish tradition that prophecy cannot occur outside the Land of Israel.[4]

RETURN

Soon after the Babylonians' destroyed the First Jewish Commonwealth in 586 BCE, Cyrus of Persia conquered the Babylonian Empire. In 538, he ordered the restoration of the Judean community and permitted the Jewish exiles to return to their homeland. Although life in Babylon was more affluent and cosmopolitan, a good number of Jews chose to return to Judea, to rebuild the Temple and renew Jewish life there. They completed the Second Temple (in the same spot as Solomon's Temple) in 516 BCE and reconstructed the walls of Jerusalem around 440 under Nehemiah's leadership. Another leader, Ezra, later emigrated from Babylon and succeeded in installing much of the Torah as the law of the Land. The story of this return has been preserved in the biblical books of Nehemiah and Ezra.

One hundred years later, Alexander of Macedonia conquered the Persian Empire that included Judea and spread Greek culture throughout the region. The interaction between Jewish and Hellenistic cultures that took place in Judea became another of the great cornerstones of the development of

Western civilization.[5] The northern region of the Jewish kingdom became known at this time as Samaria, and was centered in the city of Nablus (*Shechem* in Hebrew). The story of the Good Samaritan found in Christian Scripture (Luke 10:25–37) reflects the tension that existed even three hundred years later between Jewish life around Jerusalem and Jewish life to the north. The biblical parable describes the Samaritan from the north as having different values from the Jerusalemite priests to his south.

After Alexander died, Judea came under the political influence of the Seleucids of Mesopotamia to the east, and the Ptolemids in Egypt to the south, who allowed the Jews relative freedom in domestic affairs. They allowed a Jewish administration of priests, religious leaders, and elders to govern. This began to change when the Seleucids felt pressure from the expanding Roman Empire around 175 BCE. At that time, the Seleucid ruler, Antiochus IV, plundered the precious metals in the Temple and attempted to introduce statues, pagan rituals, and pig sacrifices into the Temple in 167 BCE. Most Jews found this sacrilege intolerable and rebelled under a small group known as the Maccabees ("hammers"). The Maccabees were led by Mattathias and his son Judah, and based themselves in the village of Modi'in. In December of 165, they succeeded in purifying the profaned Temple and forcing the reversal of Antiochus' policies. The Jewish people commemorate this victory with the holiday of Hanukkah—the Festival of Lights—a minor festival that has become a major holiday for Jews around the world. In Israel today, Hanukkah is particularly popular. Israelis visit Modi'in regularly and see Hanukkah as a symbol of political independence and a precedent for Jewish cultural and military self-defense.

ESSENES, PHARISEES, AND JESUS

Despite the Hanukkah victory, however, Hellenistic values continued to influence Jewish life in Judea. This was true among Mattathias's priestly descendents, who were known as Hasmoneans because they came from the region of Hasmon. They later ascended the monarchy and together with Judea's political and financial elite, they strengthened the process of Hellenization. As a result, dissenting religious groups sprang up. One group was the Essenes, an ascetic sect that withdrew from urban society and Jerusalem and lived in the Judean desert near the Dead Sea. The famous Dead Sea Scrolls come from the Essene community, and many historians believe that the monastic and ascetic attitudes of the Essenes influenced early Christianity.[6]

A second group was the Sadducees, primarily the wealthy aristocratic priesthood. The Pharisees, the third and largest group, were religiously opposed to the power and rites of the priests. They emphasized study and interpretation of the Bible, and developed a rich body of legal and homiletic interpretative literature around biblical texts. These teachings and literature later became the foundation of rabbinic Judaism that Jews practice today. The Pharisaic form of religious life and spiritual power was more democratic and open to all Jews. The priesthood and priestly rituals, by contrast, were confined to the sons of priests.

Jesus grew up in this Pharisaic religious culture. Many of his teachings, recorded in Christian Scripture, are near exact parallels to Pharisaic rabbinic teachings. Most famously, Jesus' statements in Matthew 22:39 and Luke 10:27, citing Leviticus 19's "Love your neighbor as yourself" as the most important commandment, mirror statements by two classic Pharisaic authorities, Rabbi Hillel and Rabbi Akiva.[7] For this reason, many Christian scholars study early rabbinic Judaism and life in Judea at the time of Jesus to obtain a fuller understanding of Jesus' teachings and religious life. Today, a significant number of Christian clergy and laypersons have decided to live in Israel to experience more directly the cultural, religious, and geographic realities of Jesus' life. Christian churches, institutes, schools, and even communities are located throughout Israel, particularly in or near Jerusalem. As we will see later, this Christian presence in the Jewish State may be the key to Christians' remaining in the Middle East, given that nowadays there is a general exodus of Christians from Muslim lands in the region.

DESTRUCTION, EXILE, AND MEMORY

The advancing Roman Empire eventually turned Judea and its Jews into a vassal of Rome. In 37 BCE, the Romans ended the Jewish Hasmonean dynasty and installed Herod as king of Judea. Herod was not a Jew but an Idumean from south of Judea. Because he curried favor with Rome, the emperor allowed him to become the most powerful Roman ruler in the East. Herod succeeded in vastly reducing Jewish independent rule and the power of the Sanhedrin judiciary, and he built cities like Caesarea (named after Caesar), and fortresses like Herodian and Masada; he also enlarged the Temple in Jerusalem. Once again, these sites are important parts of contemporary Israeli geography and culture. Judaism's holiest site today is Jerusalem's Western Wall, part of the retaining wall to the Temple Mount built by Herod.

His successor, Herod the Tetrarch, ruled during the life of Jesus from 4 BCE to 39 CE, and he killed many of the Jewish charismatic leaders, including John the Baptist. Because of this political divide, relations between the Jewish population and

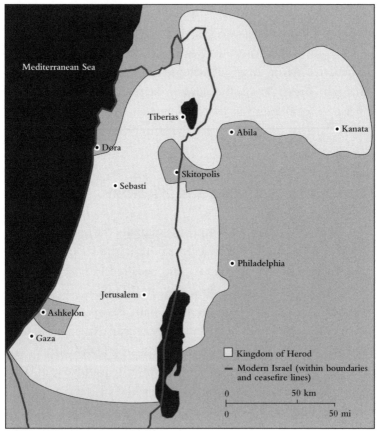

Kingdom of Herod: 30 BCE to 70 CE

the Roman authorities deteriorated rapidly; in 6 CE Rome made Judea into a province governed by Roman procurators. Pontius Pilate was the most famous. He was procurator over Judea from 26 CE to 36 CE and presided over the execution of Jesus. Pilate ruled harshly, killing a record number of Jews using the Roman method of crucifixion. This brutal reign continued under Pilate's successors until the Jews revolted in 66. The revolt ended in 70 when the Romans destroyed Jerusalem and its national symbol of national independence, the Second Temple.

With the Temple's destruction, the center of Jewish religious life moved from the priesthood in Jerusalem to Yavneh to the south, where the popular Pharisaic leaders convened to develop rabbinic Judaism and adapt Jewish law to life without Temple rituals. The loss of the Temple was a trauma, but recovery was possible through rabbinic legislation that enabled Jews to maintain national and religious continuity. During this period local synagogues assumed prominence.

The Jewish-Roman tensions continued, however, and led to repeated uprisings. When Rome decided to rebuild Jerusalem as a Roman city dedicated to the pagan god Jupiter in 132, a full-scale revolt broke out. Rome finally crushed the messianic Bar Kochba in 135, expelling all Jews from Jerusalem and deporting one out of every two Jews from Judea. Many Jews were sold as slaves throughout the empire. Between 70 and 135, the Romans killed approximately 600,000 Judean Jews; after the revolt, Jerusalem became a pagan city with a statue of Hadrian in its center. The Romans prohibited circumcision and the study of Torah, and they changed the name of the province from Judea to Palestina, a name derived from the Jewish people's arch enemy, the Philistines. In other words, the Romans did everything possible to remove traces of the Jewish people and Judaism from the province.

Although the Romans destroyed the Second Temple and later exiled most of the Jewish people from its land, they failed to sever the deep connection between the Jewish people and its homeland. Despite Roman attempts, Jews have succeeded in maintaining a continuous—if tenuous—presence in Palestine for the last 2,000 years,[8] and the Jews that were forced to leave were determined never to forget their homeland. They created living traditions for their daily religious and domestic lives that reminded them of Jerusalem's destruction, their exile, and most importantly, the hope of returning to Israel as a free and independent people. The talmudic Rabbis taught that, "One who lives outside the Land of Israel lives as if he has no God" (Babylonian Talmud, *Ketubot* 110a). Many Jews today regularly study the Mishnah, which emphasizes the spiritual and ritual holiness of Jerusalem and the Holy Land. For nearly 2,000 years Jews have prayed facing Jerusalem, and they have mourned, on the ninth day of the Jewish month of Av, the destruction of both Temples and the fall of Jerusalem. To this day, when a Jewish couple is married, they break a glass at their wedding ceremony to commemorate the destruction of the Temples. Many Jews even leave a wall or corner of their homes unfinished to symbolize and remind them of the destruction of Jerusalem.

The rabbis who fashioned Jewish liturgy incorporated prayers for the rebuilding of the Land and the return to Zion, which many Jews recite three times every day, as well as a blessing for "God who will rebuild Jerusalem in His mercy," which is recited during the Jewish grace after every meal. Jews continued to celebrate Tu B'Shevat (the fifteenth day of the Hebrew month of Shevat) as Jewish Arbor Day—the onset of spring in Israel, when the first buds on fruit trees appear. Although Tu B'Shevat occurs during the winter in America, Jews there and all over the world remind themselves that it is spring in their ancient homeland, where the time is ripe for both botanical and spiritual flowering to begin anew. Finally, the great hope for Jews returning to their homeland is expressed every year when Jews celebrate Passover. The famous Passover meal, known as the seder, which celebrates the Exodus and freedom from Egyptian slavery, ends with its participants proclaiming "Next year in Jerusalem!" Jews also announce this at the end of the holiest day of the Jewish calendar, Yom Kippur, the Day of Atonement. These prayers and traditions became central to Jewish life and kept the dream of a return to Jewish national self-determination in the hearts of the Jewish people from the time of the Roman expulsion in the first and second centuries.

PART II

A PEOPLE AND ITS GOD IN EXILE

If I forget you, O Jerusalem,
let my right hand wither;
let my tongue stick to my palate
if I cease to think of you,
if I do not elevate Jerusalem in memory
even at my happiest hour.

—PSALM 137:5

4

LOSS OF PLACE AND JEWISH LIFE IN CHRISTIAN EUROPE

THE SHIFT AWAY FROM PALESTINE

ROME'S DESTRUCTION of the Second Jewish Commonwealth and the loss of Jewish sovereignty in 70 CE transformed the Jewish people and Judaism. Geographically, many Jews remained in Palestine, but the center of Jewish life began to shift to lands in the Diaspora, where Jews lived as a dispersed minority population among other cultures. Palestinian Rabbis continued to create, even producing an impressive compendium of Jewish oral law called the Mishnah in 200 CE, and later its elaboration in the form of the Palestinian and Babylonian Talmuds.[1] Yet the shift of Jewish life to the Diaspora was inevitable after the destruction of Jerusalem and the Temple. The fact that the version of the Talmud produced by the Babylonian Rabbis around 400 CE assumed greater prominence than the Jerusalem Talmud attests to this pattern.

Jews were also forced to change their aspirations from creating a moral and religious national society to building a culture that could safeguard the Jewish identity of their minority communities. In other words, in the Diaspora, Jewish survival became the predominant concern. Because of the conditions of exile, Judaism had to develop an inward-looking defensive orientation

45

both for small Jewish communities and for individual Jews. Loss of land and independence forced Judaism itself into exile.

Immediately after the fall of Judea, the Jewish community of Egypt exercised powerful influence on the Jewish people, but Egyptian leadership gradually gave way to the Babylonian Jewish community so that by the fourth century, Babylon had became the focal point for world Jewry.

In the West, the Jews of the Roman Empire had uncertain but generally favorable legal status. However, when Christianity became the official religion of the empire early in the fourth century, the Jews' fate began to decline severely. By that time, Christianity had developed a competitive and hostile view of Jews and Judaism. Soon after Paul brought Christianity to the gentiles of the Roman Empire, Jewish influence on the church dwindled rapidly. Christians saw Judaism as a rival for religious truth and the biblical promises. Because of this theological rivalry, the original positive identification of the first Jewish Christians with the Jewish people was later shattered. Moreover, throughout the Roman Empire this rivalry tended to strengthen the prejudices about Jews that the empire's new converts to Christianity already held.

Theologically, the early church fathers began teaching that Christians displaced Jews from the covenantal relationship with God because Jews were unwilling to accept Jesus as the Messiah. This replacement idea, known as supersessionism, was the prevalent Christian teaching about Jews and Judaism from the third century until the late twentieth century. It maintained that God totally rejected the Jewish people after Jesus and led to the second, widespread teaching of the perpetual wandering Jew. This conception of Jews was so deep-seated in Christian culture that a popular houseplant, the wandering Jew, was named after it.

Christian supersessionist theology taught that because Christianity replaced Judaism, Jews lost rights to their biblical homeland. As punishment for rejecting and crucifying Jesus, Jews were condemned by God to live in misery and humiliation throughout Christian societies, and this misery functioned as an eternal sign of the Jews' blindness and stubborn sinfulness.[2] In the third century, church authorities such as Eusebius of Caesarea, Hippolytus of Rome, and Cyprian of Carthage taught this theology. The doctrine came to its fullest and most popular expression in the writings of Augustine in the fourth century. In his book *City of God*, Augustine described Jewish misery as the will of God; the Jews' public humiliation served as a "negative witness" that all the world might see to the truth of Christianity. Jews, says Augustine several times in his book, should "have their back bent down always."[3] Augustinian doctrine persisted until the nineteenth century and was accurately labeled "the teaching of contempt" by the twentieth-century historian Jules Isaac.[4]

These ideas spawned an entire genre of Christian theological writing known as the *Adversus Judaeos* (against the Jews) tradition. This literature molded the social, religious, and cultural attitudes of Christians toward Jews in Europe from the third century until today. It is easy to see how this church literature led from attitudes about Judaism directly to negative Christian behavior toward Jews themselves. Historians and Christian scholars have documented how the teaching of contempt encouraged persistent forms of social and religious anti-Semitism all over Europe down through the ages. Legally, it provided the basis for imposing political and social inferiority on Jews living in Christian countries. During the worst times of the Middle Ages, these *Adversus Judaeos* ideas triggered physical attacks, blood libels, and murders of Jews, particularly during the Crusades and the period from the eleventh to the fourteenth centuries.[5]

However, it is wrong to think that Jewish life in Christian Europe before the modern era consisted only of persecution,

The Street of the Jews
Frankfurt, Germany

suffering, forced conversions, and discrimination. There were periods when relative tolerance prevailed and when there was pragmatic cooperation between Jews and Christians, particularly in commercial relations. Autonomous Jewish communities often coexisted in a calm relationship with the larger and politically dominant Christian population.

Yet, it is undeniable that the general story of Jewish life in premodern Christian Europe contains two broad themes. First, Jews were considered foreign and inferior. As the only non-Christians in Europe, Jews were the classic "other" in Christian lands and were forced to the margins of society—politically, socially, and culturally. They were restricted legally and economically. To enforce social isolation from the Christian residents of the city, Jews were often physically confined to separate living areas—Jewish quarters or "ghettos." The term "ghetto" was first applied to the Jewish neighborhood of Venice in 1516, but Jews were forcibly segregated from Christians long before, such as in parts of Germany in the twelfth and thirteenth centuries, Sicily and Angers in the fourteenth century, and Madrid and Valencia, Spain, in the fifteenth century. There was also a Jewish ghetto in Rome founded in 1555.[6] Second, Jews and their communities were denied security and roots in the lands where they resided. They were frequently expelled by rulers from cities in which they had lived for hundreds of years and compelled to migrate to other countries. If theology taught that God decreed that Jews must be homeless, medieval European authorities ensured that Jews would not have a permanent home in their countries. The theological categories of social inferiority and homelessness became the dominant real-life experiences for the Jews of Europe between the twelfth and mid-twentieth centuries. And through all those years of exile and wandering, Jews continued to pray three times a day for their return to Zion, the biblical homeland.

Marginalization and Limitation

To understand Jewish marginalization and social inferiority in medieval European life, we can look at the pronouncements of Pope Innocent III at the beginning of the thirteenth century, when the papacy had reached the height of its political power. Innocent III had no intention of destroying the Jews of Western Europe since they served as negative witnesses to Christianity, but he insisted that Jews be merely a "tolerated subject." He enacted anti-Jewish laws and urged they be strictly enforced so that the repression of Jews would be a horrible example to any Christians who had doubts about the truth of Christianity. Among other things, Innocent legislated that Jews wear different clothing from Christians, be prohibited from having sexual relations with Christians, not appear in public from Good Friday through Easter Sunday, and be barred from holding public office.[7]

As a result of Innocent's pronouncements, a number of European states legislated that Jews wear the "badge of shame."[8] This discriminatory practice persisted in some parts of Italy well into the eighteenth century, where Jews were forced to wear a yellow Star of David on their clothing.

Jews were often viewed as inhuman, and many Europeans believed that Jews practiced satanic and brutal rituals. One popular belief was that Jews kidnapped Christian children and killed them to use their blood for making the unleavened bread called matzo used by Jews during the Passover holiday. Known as the blood libel, this periodically led to executions and massacres by residents in England, France, and Italy in the twelfth and thirteenth centuries. The blood libel became so popular among the laity that Pope Gregory X had to issue a Papal Bull in 1272 to discredit these false charges. Unfortunately, the blood libel against Jews persisted, and the accusations reappeared later, in Hungary and Russia, as late as at the end of the nineteenth century.

In 1348 Jews were also accused of poisoning the wells of Europe and causing the bubonic plague, or Black Death. This fabrication was widely believed by the residents of Germany, Switzerland, and Italy, all of whom were desperate for an explanation of the plague. The accusations led to the killing of thousands of Jews from two hundred towns in the Rhine Valley.[9] The willingness to believe that Jews committed these heinous acts indicates how isolated and foreign Jews were in the minds of the European Christians.

Jews did not fare significantly better under the Protestants during and after the Reformation of the sixteenth century. Initially Martin Luther believed that the Jews would follow him when he broke from the Catholic Church. However, when he discovered that the Jews of the German Empire would not convert to his religion of Protestant Reform, he turned bitterly against them. Here is what the leader of the Reformation wrote in his infamous essay, "Concerning the Jews and Their Lies":

> What should we Christians do with that rejected and accursed people the Jews, whom we cannot suffer because they are among us and we know so many of their lies, abusing and curses?... I shall offer my faithful suggestion:
>
> First, that we burn their synagogues with fire; and what cannot be burnt shall be buried with earth....
>
> Secondly it is necessary to uproot and destroy their houses in the same way ... in order that they know that they are not lords in our land ... but in exile and captivity
>
> There is room for apprehension, to be sure, that they are liable to harm us.... Let us therefore use the simple

wisdom of other peoples like those of France, Spain and Bohemia ... and expel them from the land forever.[10]

Luther's sixteenth-century anti-Jewish essay has provided a rich source for late medieval and modern anti-Semites alike. However, although Lutherans around the world continue to revere Luther himself, in 1995, the evangelical Lutheran Church in America repudiated his anti-Semitic statements as well as all anti-Semitism.

EXPULSIONS AND WANDERINGS

Because Jews were seen as outsiders and denied roots in mainstream society, their experience during the Middle Ages was too frequently the story of persecution, expulsion, and subsequent migrations to other lands, where Jews where forced to start life (and the cycle of anti-Semitism) anew. Jews were invited to live in countries such as Austria, Poland, Hungary, and Lithuania, usually to raise the economic conditions of those lands, but in times of intolerance or crisis, they were left unprotected by law or authorities.

In 1016, the Jewish communities of the Crimea were expelled and forced to flee to Alexandria, Constantinople, and more northern Russian cities. In 1095, Pope Urban II proclaimed a crusade to rescue Jerusalem from Muslim conquerors. Some crusaders were pious, but others were adventurers and criminals. En route from England and France to the Holy Land, some of them reasoned:

> We are going to seek the House of the Weak and Perished and to exact vengeance from the Ishmaelites; yet here are the Jews dwelling in our midst whose forefathers slew him and crucified him without reason. First let us take

vengeance on them and destroy them as a people, so that
the name of Israel shall no longer be remembered.[11]

As a result of the First Crusade, thousands of German Jews
were massacred, and the Jewish communities of Speyer,
Worms, Mayence, and Cologne in the Rhine Valley were
destroyed.

Jews had lived in France for over a thousand years when
Phillip Augustus came to power in 1179. In order to raise
money and fight off powerful barons in his land, he imprisoned
all Jews in France, releasing them only after they paid exorbi-
tant ransoms in 1180. The next year, he annulled Jewish loans
to Christians if Christians paid 20 percent of the loan to him.
Finally, in 1182 he confiscated all Jewish property and land, and
drove Jews out of every place he ruled. Jews were invited back
into France toward the end of the twelfth century, but most
were expelled again in 1306. After massacres there in 1348, the
creativity of medieval French Jewry ended.[12]

Jews were expelled from England in 1290; most went to
France and Germany. Jews were not allowed to return to
England until the second half of the seventeenth century. At
the same time that Jews were forced out of England, the Jewish
communities of the Kingdom of Naples were almost entirely
destroyed. To induce Jews there to convert, the authorities
offered to remit the taxes of almost 1,500 families if they
would become Christians. Massacres continued, and by 1294,
all the Jewish communities of southern Italy, which included
more than 10,000 people, were destroyed.[13]

Two hundred years later, in 1492, King Ferdinand and
Queen Isabella expelled from Spain all Jews who refused to
convert. The expulsion was motivated partly by greed and
partly by the intensified feeling of Christian triumph by the
people who had just won a crusade against the Moors. (Jews

were not considered part of the Spanish nation.) Mostly, however, it was motivated by Isabella's religious zeal. With the stroke of a pen, the Spanish monarchs put an end to the largest and most influential Jewish settlement in Europe. About 200,000 Jews were forced to leave Spain after having had to sell their land for low prices and not being allowed to leave with their gold and silver. About 100,000 went to Portugal and Turkey, some to North Africa, and others to Rome and Naples.[14] Later, in 1497, many Portuguese Jews were forcibly converted.

Because the Jewish communities of Western Europe were ruined or expelled in the fourteenth century, Casimir the Great of Poland invited Jews to his kingdom as merchants and intermediaries. A century later, the number of Polish Jews had reached 500,000. The Jewish communities there were stable for two hundred years, but when Poland experienced constitutional crises in the mid-seventeenth century, those Jewish communities experienced rapid decline. Many Polish Jews then migrated to Romania and Russia, early in the eighteenth century.

Jews were expelled from Berlin in the sixteenth century, but in the next century, Frederick William was eager to improve economic conditions devastated by the Thirty Years War (1618–48). He encouraged Polish Jews to travel and trade in his lands, and in 1670, he formally invited Jews who had just been expelled from Vienna to live in Brandenburg. These Jews had to pay an annual protection tax as well as a special tax in order to get married.[15] Homelessness and marginalization proved to be tragic realities for European Jews in exile. Diaspora suffering was eased a bit by the yearning that Jews expressed constantly in daily prayers, rituals, and holy days to return to their homeland, which would offer both spiritual rewards and physical security But the resulting insecurity and suffering from the eleventh to the eighteenth centuries made a profound stamp on Jewish life, religion, and worldview.

THE IMPACT OF EXILE ON JUDAISM AND JEWISH VALUES

Because Jews were excluded from the political and social mainstream in medieval Europe, they could not participate in the national and moral development of European culture. As a result, Jewish life turned inward, and Jews became increasingly focused on what they in their insulated Jewish communities could influence: the study of sacred texts, the intimacy of Jewish family life at home, and synagogue practices and rituals. As outsiders, Jews found it impossible to implement in wider society the lofty covenantal and prophetic values of social justice, peace, improving the world (known in Hebrew as *tikkun olam*), eliminating poverty and promoting social equality, and universal human dignity. Hence these ideals receded into the background of Jewish life and religion. Sabbath and holidays, Torah study, dietary laws, and prayer came to dominated Jewish life in the Diaspora.

In addition, because Jews were the weaker party in Christian-Jewish relations and were frequently victimized by European institutions and authorities, Jews developed an "ethic of suspicion" as a response to gentile power. This is yet another moral and spiritual tragedy, since both the Bible (Genesis 1:27) and Judaism (Babylonian Talmud, *Mishnah Avot* 3:18) teach the ideals that all persons are created in the image of God, and that mutual dignity and appreciation should govern relations between all people, independent of religion or nationality. So the medieval European experience for Jews was indeed a curse on both physical and spiritual levels: It robbed Jews of physical security as well as the ability to naturally develop the deep national covenantal values taught by the Bible and the Rabbis of the Talmud.

5

MODERN PROMISES, STIRRINGS OF RETURN, AND THE HOLOCAUST

THE DAWN OF HOPE IN EUROPE

ENORMOUS SOCIAL AND ECONOMIC CHANGES took place in Europe during the seventeenth and eighteenth centuries. These changes altered the political structures of countries in Western and Central Europe, and transformed the lives of Christians and Jews alike. This beginning of the modern era provided hope for the improvement of Jewish life in exile.

A great amount of money poured into Europe in the seventeenth century, and this raised living standards and initiated the shift from the old agricultural and feudal economies to a mercantile or commercial economy. Rulers sought to monopolize trade and wealth, ensure a positive balance of international payments, and accumulate as much money as possible. Money became the great equalizer, forcing people's religious differences to the background of social and political importance. Religious toleration became more common because it promoted stability and was profitable.[1]

With these commercial forces at work, European rulers began to view Jews differently. Because Jews had traditionally been denied roots on European land, they had long been forced into finance and trade to survive. Jews understand commerce and provided stimulation for economies, and so they became increasingly useful to European rulers in this new age of mercantilism. Many who ruled in the Netherlands, England, France, and Prussia extended tolerance to individual Jews who were economically successful. Most European Jews still made a meager living from peddling and were confined to ghetto neighborhoods, but by the mid-1600s, a new thinking and political order had broken through: The central distinction was no longer between Christian and Jew, but between rich and poor.

Islands of tolerance slowly began to appear. Jews had been banished from England in the thirteenth century, but when a small group of Dutch Jews petitioned Oliver Cromwell, who then ruled, for permission to enter England in the middle of the seventeenth century, he granted it over the opposition of his counselors. By 1660 there were thirty-five Jewish families in London, but their numbers increased as did their rights. In the eighteenth century, Jews were officially given the right of residence and were allowed to use English courts to recover their debts. They integrated into much of England's economic life, and Jewish financiers and merchants were gradually tolerated by the elite of English society.

Dutch rulers also wished to promote trade during this period and accepted petitions for Jews to enter. Jews living in the Netherlands were not confined to ghettos and they found a semblance of equality before the law.

In the late seventeenth century, the spirit of reason also began to rise in Europe. The middle class used rationalism to criticize the old institutions like royalty, bishops, and land barons that had monopolized wealth and status in their societies. A number of thinkers began to question as well the value of ancient persecutions, discriminations, and ghettoization. However, the new faith in reason applied to Jews and their exceptional status (which was known as "the Jewish problem") very cautiously. In his *Letter Concerning Toleration* of 1689, the famous British political philosopher John Locke extended tolerance to Jews in England, but he still considered their religion "abominable." Some French philosophers continued to see Jews as backward and inferior people. Denis Diderot, author of the famed *Encyclopédie,* saw Jews as innately bigoted. The famous Voltaire, a major figure in destroying the old French regime, described Jews as "an ignorant and barbarous people, who have long exercised the most sordid avarice and detestable superstition."[2]

These new secular philosophers were anticlerical and anti-Christian. They identified Jews with the old order and church abuse, since Christianity sprang from Judaism. Nevertheless, the rationalists gradually began to realize that ignorance, superstition, and clannishness were not innate Jewish traits. Exceptional Jews like the intellectually gifted Moses Mendelssohn in mid-eighteenth century Germany helped convince enlightened thinkers that Jews and Christians could share a common—if secular—humanity and that it was logical to extend that fellowship to all Jews, not merely to the wealthy and the remarkably learned.

On the eve of the French Revolution of 1789, the majority of Jews were still locked out of the mainstream of European life. They had no rights of free movement, and they were confined to slums and prohibited from entering the halls of Western culture. Yet mercantilism, capitalism, and rationalism had cracked the old order, and modern-looking Europeans were more receptive to letting Jews out of the intellectual, economic and political ghettos in which they had been confined for close to eight hundred years.

REVOLUTION AND EMANCIPATION

The economic crisis in France in 1789 led to the formation of the National Assembly and the idea of a constitution for

France. Inspired by the democratic principles of America's Declaration of Independence, the assembly wrote a prefix to the French Constitution called "The Declaration of the Rights of Man." (The idea of human rights may seem obvious to many of us in the twenty-first century, but it was a new and radical concept in 1789.) The declaration proclaimed the principle of equality of all people regardless of station of birth and, by implication, of all religious identities; all citizens had the right to participate directly in the national government of France. This transformed the French social order and eliminated medieval anachronisms like unequal taxation, feudalism, and guilds. It drastically reduced the power of the French Catholic church and granted civil and political rights to Protestants—but not yet to the 40,000 French Jews who remained second-class citizens.

THE DREAM OF EQUALITY

The spirit of humanitarian reason gathered strength. The French Revolution's motto was "Liberty, Fraternity, Equality." Early in 1791, Jews were relieved of paying special taxes, and by the end of the year, French Jews were granted full rights of citizenship. Jews entered the French army and public schools, and believed they could become patriotic Frenchmen while remaining faithful practicing Jews. Despite equality before the law, however, the traditional social resentment against Jews continued. Royalists accused them of wanting to destroy Christianity, and peasants resented owing money to Jewish businessmen.

Partially to appease those unhappy with Jewish citizenship, Emperor Napoleon summoned Jewish notables to Paris in 1806 and demanded answers to twelve questions like "In the eyes of Jews, are Frenchmen not of the Jewish faith brothers or strangers?" and "Do Jews born in France consider France their country?" Jews were still suspected of being dangerous aliens, and Napoleon challenged the Jews' loyalty. In effect, he demanded that Jews give up their corporate identity as the people of Israel for their allegiance to the new French nation. The notables answered affirmatively, but Napoleon remained unconvinced. In 1807 he summoned a group of rabbis ("the Great Sanhedrin," named after the biblical Jewish court) and demanded that Jews forever renounce the idea of separate nationhood and their traditional hope for a return to their ancient homeland. Eager for security and acceptance, the Sanhedrin agreed; Napoleon's commissioner wrote that "today Jews ceased to be a people and remained only a religion."[3] Nevertheless, Jews continued to pray for and dream of the return to Zion and the restoration of Jewish nationhood.

Napoleon wanted to become emperor of Europe, and by 1807 he had conquered Belgium, Holland, Germany, Prussia, and Austria. Throughout his conquests, he extended similar citizenship rights to the Jews of those lands. Yet opposition from German leaders remained. Johann Fichte, a well-known German thinker of the time, said, "The only way by which I see civil rights can be given to them [the Jews] is to cut off all their heads in one night and set new ones on their shoulders that would not contain a single Jewish idea."[4] Nevertheless, as Napoleon conquered one German state after another, he dismantled the ghettos and emancipated the Jews of those territories. In 1812, the Jews of Prussia received a grant of emancipation. Only in some parts of Central Europe, in Austria, Hungary, and Bohemia, were Jews forced to continue to live as tolerated non-Europeans for a few more generations.

For the Jews, the modern era meant emancipation: the end to their segregated and oppressed status, the freedom to integrate into mainstream society, and a precious equality before the law with their Christian neighbors. But the price of emancipation was high, as one famous statement of the time indicates: "To the Jews as individuals, everything; to the Jews as a nation, nothing."[5]

Anti-Semitism, Confinement, and Poverty in Eastern Europe

Enlightenment came more slowly to Eastern Europe, where the old ways, despotic rulers, and anti-Semitism still ruled in Russia, Poland, and Lithuania. During the eighteenth century, Jews were still viewed as infidels and prisoners of Christianity by the Russian and Greek Orthodox churches and by tsars like Peter I and Catherine II. Because of this view, Jews were not permitted to live in Russia. "I prefer to see in our midst nations professing Islam or paganism rather than Jews. It is my endeavor to eradicate evil, not multiply it," proclaimed Peter.[6] In 1762, Catherine permitted foreigners to settle in Russia, "except the Jews."

Russia annexed Lithuania in 1795, however, and soon afterward, Poland was partitioned with the regions of Warsaw and eastern Poland falling under the rule of Tsar Alexander I. As a result, Russia inherited one million Jews by the beginning of the nineteenth century, and by the end of that century, the number of Jews had swelled to more than five million under tsarist oppression in Russia and Poland. To prevent Jews from contaminating native Russians, Jews were confined by decree to a small area of territory along the border of former Poland called the Pale of Settlement. In effect, the Pale was a vast ghetto. This decree imposed an enormously heavy economic and political burden on Jews and confined them to an intellectual prison that sealed them off from mainstream Russian culture. In the same century when the Jews of France, Germany,

and England began to experience improvement in their economic, political, and social status, the Jews of the Russian Pale
were systematically driven out of the countryside and from
professional guilds and reduced to peddling and a pariah status.
Because Alexander I felt threatened by Napoleon's army
and enlightened ideas, he refused to allow any political or economic progress for Russian Jews. Alexander was determined to
destroy national Jewish identity, and in 1804 he tried to enact
reactionary legislation that stripped Jews of any communal
authority and promoted devious Jewish conversion to
Christianity by inducing Jews to enter Russian public education that was "suffused with Christian spirit." This same legislation revoked any Jewish leases on land, denied Jews the right
to operate taverns, and expelled Jews from villages and hamlets
into larger towns and cities. In other words, Alexander
attempted to undermine their livelihoods and increase their
ghettoization. Even the Russian Constitution proved to be a
nightmare for Jews.[7] When Napoleon's army left Russia in
defeat in the beginning of the nineteenth century, Jews lost all
hope of enlightened reform.

Nicholas I succeeded Alexander in 1825, and when he
crushed the Polish revolt against his rule, he treated Jews bru-
tally. He enacted legislation to draft Jews at age twelve into the
Russian army for a period of thirty-one years. Conscription for
Jewish boys at that age meant death or forced conversion. The
children were frequently beaten, starved, or whipped to go to
church services. Sometimes they were forcibly baptized; those
who refused drowned in the Volga River. There were numerous instances of mass suicide by drowning at baptismal ceremonies.[8] In the 1840s, the government recommended secular
Russian education for Jews, again for the purpose of conversion. Jews who understood this refused to comply, which drove
them even further away from Russian culture and intensified

their status as aliens. There was no way for Jews to remain Jews and live with dignity or security under the tsars.

By 1855, there were three million Jews living in the Pale under Alexander II. He opened up the interior of Russia to "useful elements of the Jewish population"—successful merchants, university graduates, and skilled artisans—but this in turn lowered the economy of the Jewish peddlers and shopkeepers left in the Pale. Ten years later, Alexander halted all reforms, and in 1871, his commission on the Jews recommended abolishing all traces of separate Jewish identity by closing Jewish schools, self-help communal organizations, and anything else that fostered Jewish communal cohesion.

Toward the end of the nineteenth century, more than five million Jews were crowded into the small area of the Pale. Most were poor like the milkman Tevye, a character in Scholem Aleichem's stories who was made famous in the play *Fiddler on the Roof.* They lived in small villages, like Anatevka or Kasrilevska, described here by the writer Maurice Samuel:

> Kasrielevky is like any one of a hundred Jewish or half-Jewish centres in old Russia. The town itself is a jumble of wooden houses clustering higgledy-piggledy about a market-place at the foot of a hill. All around is the spaciousness of mighty Russia, but Kasrielevky is as crowded as a slum, is in fact a slum…. Most of the market-place was occupied by peddlers, hangers-on, parodies of commission men, women with a basket of eggs or a bundle of old clothes. And the richest Jew in Kasrielevky could be bought out on a lower margin of four figures. Rich or poor, peddlers or artisans, their livelihood was from the market-place, and from semi-annual fairs. It depends, naturally, on what you call a living…. Yerechmiel Moses, the Hebrew teacher, blind in one eye and short-sighted in the

other, used to wear spectacles without lenses. Asked why, he would answer triumphantly: "Well it's better than nothing, isn't it?"[9]

Despite the poverty and anti-Semitic discrimination, Jewish life was dominated by tradition. Crime was low, and violence within the Jewish community was quite rare. Traditional religious observance provided structure to ghetto life and gave Jews pride and stable moral values. There were numerous charitable agencies in the Pale, from soup kitchens to poorhouses to dispensaries—necessary, since by 1880, one out of every five residents in the Pale relied on charity to survive.[10]

From 1880 until the First World War in 1914, pogroms and "spontaneous" outbursts of rioting increased against Russian Jewish communities. In 1881, thousands of Jews were killed in a series of particularly brutal pogroms that the Russian government instigated throughout the Pale after the assassination of Tsar Alexander II. The medieval accusations of blood libel and ritual murder resurfaced from time to time during that era, one of the most famous being the 1911 case against Mendel Beilis in Russia. As Russian and Slavic culture intensified, so did incitement against the Jewish "foreigners." Pogroms also broke out in Romania, the Baltic countries, and Warsaw. The surge of anti-Semitism and enforced poverty at the end of the nineteenth century led more than 2,000,000 Eastern European Jews during this period to flee to America, and another 500,000 to escape to other lands in the West and Palestine in the Middle East. They migrated in search of hope, dignity, and acceptance.[11]

THE DREAM REAWAKENS

The Jews who left Eastern Europe for Palestine at the end of the nineteenth century joined more than 25,000 Jews who had lived in the Holy Land for hundreds of years. Although the majority of Jews between the years 1000 and 1900 lived in exile in Europe, they never forgot their ancient biblical homeland and the idea of independent Jewish nationhood. Every year religious Jews read from the Book of Lamentations that mourns the loss of Jerusalem and forced exile from the Land. Jewish hopes and prayers during this period were best captured by Rabbi Judah Halevi's confession in his famous eleventh-century poem: "I am in the West, but my heart is in the East."

A number of Jews went to Palestine after being expelled from Spain in 1492. By the middle of the 1700s, there were more than ten thousand Jews living in the religious city of Safed in northern Palestine, and by the beginning of the 1800s, that number had swelled to over twenty thousand.[12] In 1854, Jews in Jerusalem constituted the city's largest religious group, and by 1870, they were the absolute majority.[13] Jews have continued to be the majority in Jerusalem ever since. During that time, Palestine was a poor and largely uninhabited backwater of the Ottoman Empire. The area was undeveloped, and the inhabitants were mostly peasants and poor Arab farmers, many of whom had arrived recently from Arab lands to the East. There was no unity or national identity among the non-Jewish population, whose allegiance was to the Ottoman Empire.[14]

Well before the outbreak of severe anti-Semitism in Europe at the end of the nineteenth century, Jewish thinkers understood that Emancipation in the West meant the end of the biblical, religious, and cultural ideal of Jews as a distinct people. In 1862, the emancipated secular Jew Moses Hess wrote in his book *Rome and Jerusalem* that there is no such thing as a universal religion or universal culture. Therefore in an era when nationalism was forming and Germany and Italy each became unified into nations, Jews faced the choice of either losing their Jewish identity by assimilating into a foreign culture or restoring their distinctive national identity in their own country centered around Jerusalem. Hess believed that rational and enlightened Frenchmen, Italians, and Germans would understand this and support Jewish national independence in Palestine. In Eastern Europe in the 1850s, Rabbis Judah Alkalai and Zvi Hirsch Kalischer both taught that the spiritual mission of the Jewish people and God's plan for sacred history demanded that Jews reconstitute themselves in the biblical homeland of Zion. Only then could they achieve national independence and redemption for the world. This was nothing other than the ancient biblical dream; only the transition from passive waiting to political activism was new. Alkalai and Kalischer stressed the religious commandment of living in the Holy Land and started funds to help Jews migrate to Palestine.

These early Zionist thinkers—both secular and religious—understood that a spiritual center in the ancient Jewish homeland was essential for the renaissance of the Jewish people. Jewish national self-determination required returning to Zion. What was the right of Frenchmen in France, Italians in Italy, and Germans in Germany was also the right of Jews as a people: national independence in their own native country.

The widespread Russian pogroms of 1881–84 shocked the educated Jews there, who expected that emancipation and acceptance into Russian culture would occur soon. When no section of Russian society defended Jews while rioting and violence ran amok, enlightened Jewish thinkers could no longer deny that anti-Semitism was deeply rooted in Russia— and likely to remain so for the future. This realization led a Jewish doctor named Leon Pinsker to analyze anti-Semitism in a clinical manner. In his 1882 pamphlet, *Auto-Emancipation*, Pinsker explained that anti-Semitism was based on the fact that Jews were unique. They were the only people in history to have survived for centuries in exile. Pinsker realized that modernity's denationalization of Jews had not solved the problem of Jew hatred but compounded it:

> Not only is he not a native in his own country, but he is also not a foreigner; he is in every truth, the stranger par excellence.... The foreigner has a claim to hospitality, which he can repay in the same coin. The Jew can make no such return; consequently he can make no claim to hospitality. The Jews are aliens who have no representatives, because they have no country.[15]

Pinsker argued that without its homeland, Jews were a spiritual people without a body. A nation without its land is like a disembodied ghost moving around inside larger society, and ghosts naturally frighten normal people. Anti-Semitism, then, is a psychological aberration—a fear of Jews. Fear quickly turns to hate, and people try to destroy what they fear. If Judeophobia was the diagnosis, the cure could only be the return of the Jewish people to their national body, their homeland. Only then, he taught, would people's fear of Jews be conquered and the disease of anti-Semitism overcome. When Jews reestablished their national sovereignty in their native land of Palestine, Jews would again be "normal"—even Jews living outside the Jewish state. Pinsker advocated setting up political organizations to purchase land in Palestine as a refuge for the Jews of Russia, Romania, and Morocco who were fleeing persecution and violence.

In the face of the pogroms, other Russian Jews came to the same conclusion. "There can be no salvation for Israel if it does not found a government of its own in the Land of Israel." This was the motto of a new organization, Chovevei Tzion (Lovers of Zion), which was founded in 1882 to promote Jewish return to Zion and "to stimulate the economic, national, and spiritual renaissance of the Hebrew people in Palestine." Similar organizations sprang up in Romania. They merged into an international organization and helped poor Jews of the East immigrate to Palestine. This migration was called *aliyah*, "going up," since Jewish tradition always considered the Land of Israel to be on a higher spiritual level than the lands of exile. The town of Petach Tikvah ("The Gate of Hope") was founded in 1878 by Jerusalem Jews, but was soon abandoned due to malaria, starvation, and other harsh conditions. However, in 1882 European Jews resettled Petach Tikvah and founded the new town of Rishon Lezion ("First in Zion"). The motto of these immigrants was "to build the land and to be built up by it." They labored in the desert, swamps, and wastelands to bring the Land of Israel back to life and to become new self-reliant Jews who were again connected to the Land and its soil. Here is how the administration of the League of Nations described the achievements of the immigrants:

> "Jewish agricultural colonies ... developed the culture of oranges.... They drained swamps. They planted eucalyptus trees. They practiced, with modern methods, all the processes of agriculture. Every traveler in Palestine is impressed by the beautiful stretches of prosperous cultivation about them."[16]

No longer would Jews be ghosts, but a normal people of flesh and blood, with dignity, security, and national character.

From the years 1880 to 1914, the Jewish population of Palestine rose from 25,000 to 85,000, with nearly the entire increase consisting of immigrants from Eastern Europe. The bloody 1903 Kishinev pogrom in Russia and the failed Russian revolution in 1905 forced more Jewish emigration.

Jewish organizations purchased most of the land that Jews developed—approximately 100,000 acres—which was owned overwhelmingly by absentee landlords.[17] Palestine, then, was largely barren, and Western officials described it as "empty," "silent," and "waste."[18] Only one tenth of the total land was cultivated in 1895.[19]

In 1880, the non-Jewish population of western Palestine[20] was about 300,000. About 57,000 were nomads who did not claim land, and 55,000 were Christians. This had been a relatively constant figure for two centuries because there was little development in the area to attract new residents. By 1918, the number had increased to approximately 500,000, much of it due to Arab migration into the area, which in turn had been stimulated by Jewish development of the land, better living conditions, and the improved local economy. This pattern of Arab immigration into Palestine on the heels of Jewish development followed until 1947. One prominent historian put it this way: "No one doubted that the Arabs had benefited from Jewish immigration. Their numbers had almost doubled between 1917 and 1940, wages had shot up, and the standard of living had risen more than anywhere else in the Middle East."[21]

THE GATHERING STORM AND THE CALL TO ZION

Dangerous signs were beginning to appear in the "enlightened" countries of Western Europe—France and Germany. In 1894, a Jewish officer in the French army, Captain Alfred Dreyfus, was charged with espionage. There was little evidence of Dreyfus's guilt, and it was widely understood that Dreyfus was accused only because he was a Jew. The French press played up the old canard of the international Jewish conspiracy, portraying Dreyfus and Jews as traitors to the French nation. The affair became public, and Dreyfus was falsely convicted and left to rot in a prison cell on Devil's Island. In 1898, the affair exploded into a public scandal. Dreyfus was eventually exonerated after seven long years, but the damage was done. France, the country that had first promised "Liberty, Equality, Fraternity" to Jews a hundred years earlier, now proved that anti-Semitism still ran deep in modern Europe and that the Enlightenment's promise of acceptance was false.

A new strain of Jew-hatred was also brewing in Germany at the end of the nineteenth century: racial anti-Semitism. It was then that the term "anti-Semitism" was first used by an Austrian scholar named Moritz Steinschneider, to name the specific phenomenon of prejudice against Jews. During the Middle Ages, Jews were seen as different because of their religion and traditions. Now, however, nationalist German writers began to propound theories regarding the racial superiority of the German folk, and the need to protect that superiority against contamination from Jews. "We should take earnest account of this degeneration to explain the decay of the German folk which is now exposed without defense to the penetration of the Jews," stated the famous composer Richard Wagner.[22] According to the popular racist ideologue Houston Chamberlain, an Englishman who moved to Germany during this period, the Jews never produced anything good—neither the Bible nor Jesus, who Chamberlain claimed was Aryan. On the contrary, Jews had a mission to pollute the earth and the German people. These writers used the cultural precedents of European Jew-hatred as a useful political tool to maintain power, but they added a racial contempt for Jews. The myth of German Aryan superiority meant defamation of non-Aryans, but the comparison between Germans and Jews became a comparison between superhuman and subhuman. Jews were portrayed, once again, as a different species that posed a threat to human culture. Though these grotesque ideas gained political popularity, they did not translate into violence or political action against Jews. They did, however, foreshadow the great horror that was to unfold for European Jews from 1933 to 1945.

An assimilated Austrian Jew named Theodor Herzl covered the Dreyfus affair for the European press. Herzl was shocked by the outbreak of anti-Semitic sentiment in liberal France and it caused him to reconsider the fate of Jews in Europe. He became a champion of Jewish national independence and in 1896 wrote a book, *The Jewish State*, advocating a sovereign Jewish homeland: "The world resounds with outcries against the Jews, and these outcries have awakened the slumbering idea," Herzl concluded. Like his Jewish brothers in Russia, he too realized that a free and independent Jewish state was the only answer to anti-Semitism. Herzl began practical political activity to galvanize economic, diplomatic, and political support for establishing a Jewish state in the ancient Jewish homeland of Zion, which was now called Palestine. He summoned the first World Zionist Congress in Basel in 1897 to begin a movement of political Zionism. Herzl wrote another important book, in 1902, called *Altneuland* (*Old-New Land*) that described his vision of a free Jewish society in Zion. This society would allow Jews to flourish and would mirror the best moral and social ideals of Western liberalism.

Other thinkers more attuned to Jewish culture, such as Asher Ginzberg (known as Ahad Ha-am), Eliezer Ben Yehudah, and Chaim Weizmann, joined the Zionist movement and stressed the redevelopment of Hebrew as the Jewish national language, Jewish self-reliance in achieving statehood, and democratic processes for the movement and the future state. After the Kishinev pogrom in 1903, where forty-five Jews were murdered and over fifteen hundred Jewish homes were destroyed, political activity quickened and there seemed to be a willingness to give Jews some territory for a homeland in Uganda, Africa. Despite the massacres occurring in Kishinev at the time, Zionists rejected the idea. Only a modern country in its ancient biblical homeland would allow the Jewish people to restore its national identity and its authentic cultural, religious, and moral values. Herzl died in 1904, but he reawakened the eternal longing for Zion and started a powerful political movement. The idea of the return to Zion continued to gather strength, and when England assumed control of Palestine from the Turks after World War I, the British foreign secretary, Lord Balfour, promised to provide a homeland in Zion for the Jewish people in his famous resolution of November 2, 1917:

> His Majesty's Government views with favour the establishment in Palestine of a national home for the Jewish people, and will use their best endeavours to facilitate the achievement of this object, it being clearly understood that nothing shall be done which may prejudice the civil and religious rights of existing non-Jewish communities in Palestine.[23]

Holocaust and Extermination

Jews had lived a painful exile in Christian Europe for more than one thousand years. It was marked by teachings of contempt, forced conversions, blood libels, ghettoization, discriminatory laws, pogroms, and expulsions. Yet none of those tragic experiences prepared the nine million Jews living in Europe and Russia in the first half of the twentieth century for the extermination about to take place from 1933 to 1945. This was Europe's Final Solution to the "Jewish question," brutal and evil on a level never experienced before by any people in history. It was the methodical annihilation of human bodies on a mass scale, the systematic slaughter of an entire people and their culture. It extinguished any hope that Jews could be safe or secure in exile under the benevolence of European rulers. Quite simply, it was a holocaust.

The devastation that became formally known as the Holocaust, or *Shoah* (Hebrew) has been well documented.[24] The near success of the Final Solution in eliminating Jews from the face of the earth is a heartbreaking story of satanic planning and meticulous execution that used the most sophisticated science and bureaucratic techniques of its day. It is a story of the readiness of tens of thousands of perpetrators to exterminate Jews; the recruitment of millions to assist in the killing operations; and the apathy of tens of millions of bystanders around the world who stood by while the slaughter took place. An outline of this tragedy of betrayal and extermination is crucial to understanding why the State of Israel plays such a crucial role in securing the future of the Jewish people, why Jews today feel existentially connected to Israel and personally obligated to safeguard her security, and why Israel plays a central role today in the self-consciousness of Jews everywhere.

By the time World War I ended, the Jews of Germany, Austria, and Hungary were more integrated into gentile society than anywhere else in the world. Although Jews were concentrated in the cities, they constituted only about 1 percent of the total German population at the beginning of the war. More than 100,000 Jews served in the German army. Of that number, 10,000 were killed in battle, and 35,000 were decorated for bravery. Jews were doctors, professors, bankers, government workers, and musicians contributing to German life and culture. But Germany's crushing defeat in the war and the harsh conditions for surrender imposed by the allies caused the German economy to collapse. It also popularized the notions of Germanic folk destiny and the militant German nationalism that nineteenth-century German writers idealized. To explain Germany's political and economic depression, Germans turned to Wagner's and Chamberlain's idea of the German race, which blamed non-Aryans for Germany's fall. Under the weight of national chaos, this racism mutated into a wild xenophobia.

Out of this instability, Adolf Hitler and his Nazi party gained control of Germany in 1933. He immediately suspended Germany's democratic institutions and began enacting his extreme political program. Hitler's anti-Semitism was the most central element in the program. It built on centuries of Christian discrimination against the Jews but raised it to a radically different level. Hitler's anti-Semitism became "raw, naked Jew-hatred, wild, undisciplined and nihilistic."[25] Above all, the Nazis demanded that Germany undergo Aryanization and cleanse itself of the "blood poisoning by the Jewish race." After only three months in power, Hitler's government succeeded in passing laws prohibiting Jews from working in government, the courts, the railroads, education, and medicine. Jewish books were burned by Nazi storm troopers, and Jewish children were removed from German schools. In September 1935, the new Nuremberg laws took away citizenship from Jews and forbade them to marry non-Jews. In April 1938, the government confiscated all Jewish money and property worth more than $2,000 per person from the 350,000 Jews remaining in Germany (out of a total German population of close to 80 million). Those who chose to leave forfeited even the $2,000 and fled penniless.

Later in 1938, Nazi anti-Semitism turned from discrimination to outright sanctioned violence. From November 9 to 10, the Nazis conducted a national pogrom. Nearly every Jewish home was attacked, and in one night (*Kristallnacht*—the night of broken glass) five hundred synagogues were burned to the ground. Jews were savagely beaten and ninety were

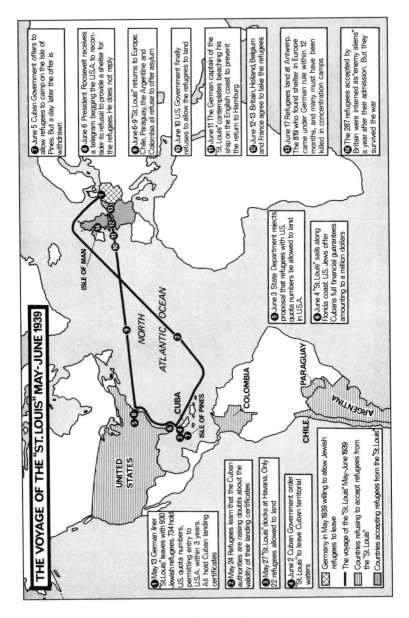

THE VOYAGE OF THE "ST. LOUIS" MAY-JUNE 1939

① May 13 German liner "St.Louis" leaves with 930 Jewish refugees. 734 hold U.S. quota numbers, permitting entry to U.S.A. within 3 years. All hold Cuban landing certificates

② May 24 Refugees learn that the Cuban authorities are raising doubts about the validity of their landing certificates

③ May 27 "St.Louis" docks at Havana. Only 22 refugees allowed to land

④ June 2 Cuban Government order "St.Louis" to leave Cuban territorial waters

⑤ June 3 State Department rejects proposal that refugees with U.S. quota numbers be allowed to land in U.S.A.

⑥ June 4 "St. Louis" sails along Florida coast. U.S. Jews offer Cubans full financial guarantees amounting to a million dollars

⑦ June 5 Cuban Government offers to allow refugees to camp on the Isle of Pines. But a day later the offer is withdrawn

⑧ June 6 President Roosevelt receives a telegram begging the U.S.A. to reconsider its refusal to provide a shelter for the refugees. He does not reply

⑨ June 6-9 "St. Louis" returns to Europe. Chile, Paraguay, the Argentine and Colombia all refuse to offer asylum

⑩ June 10 U.S. Government finally refuses to allow the refugees to land

⑪ June 11 The German captain of the "St.Louis" contemplates beaching his ship on the English coast to prevent the return to Hamburg

⑫ June 12-13 Britain, Holland, Belgium and France agree to take the refugees

⑬ June 17 Refugees land at Antwerp. The 819 who found shelter in Europe came under German rule within 12 months, and many must have been killed in concentration camps

⑭ The 287 refugees accepted by Britain were interned as "enemy aliens" a year after their admission. But they survived the war

UNITED STATES

NORTH ATLANTIC OCEAN

ISLE OF MAN

CUBA

ISLE OF PINES

COLOMBIA

PARAGUAY

ARGENTINA

CHILE

⊠ Germany in May 1939 willing to allow Jewish refugees to leave

—— The voyage of the "St. Louis" May-June 1939

▥ Countries refusing to accept refugees from the "St. Louis"

▨ Countries accepting refugees from the "St. Louis"

The Voyage of the "St. Louis" May–June 1939

murdered. Fifty thousand Jews were arrested and flung into concentration camps. The government fined the German-Jewish community for the damage—some $400 million dollars. By January 1, 1939, all Jewish businesses had been liquidated and "Aryanized."[26]

The world protested but otherwise did nothing to stop the Nazi violence. Nor were countries willing to admit Jews, even after the violence in Germany was well known. Hitler demonstrated this by allowing 930 Jews to flee Germany in May 1939 on a ship named the *St. Louis*. The ship sailed to Cuba and the United States on a "voyage of the damned," where the refugees pleaded for asylum while they were docked in Havana and off the Florida coast. Both Cuba and America refused them admission, even though 734 of the passengers held quota papers permitting them to enter temporarily. The *St. Louis* and her doomed passengers were sent back to Europe, where their pleas to Chile, Paraguay, and Argentina for asylum were also rejected. Eventually Belgium, Holland, and England admitted 819 of them in June, but within twelve months Hitler had conquered Belgium, and many of the passengers were murdered in the extermination process.

The Nazi brutality was not limited to thugs and uneducated people. Hitler recruited professors and intellectuals to substantiate his scientifically fanciful racial theories and stoke the "eternal war" between the Aryans and non-Aryans. Jews escaped when they could, and by the end of 1939, more than 350,000 Jews from Germany, Austria, and Czechoslovakia had fled to other countries. Many were the greatest scientists and intellectuals of Europe, and among them were Albert Einstein, the philosopher Martin Buber, the theologian Abraham Joshua Heschel, and the physicist Robert Oppenheimer. When Hitler took over Austria in 1938, it was the beginning of the end for the 200,000 Jews there. The Austrians quickly aided the Nazis in "cleansing" Austria of Jews. After British prime minister Neville Chamberlain appeased Hitler by ceding to him part of Czechoslovakia, the 350,000 Jews of that country were doomed. Only 35,000 managed to flee.

With Austria and Czechoslovakia under Nazi control, in 1940 Hitler conquered France, Norway, Denmark, Holland, Belgium, and Luxembourg in short order, threatening the lives of the 565,000 Jews living in those countries. Soon after, he conquered Poland (3,3000,000 Jews), the Ukraine (1,700,000 Jews), and the Baltic States (200,000 Jews), and drove deep into the Soviet Union (1,000,000 Jews). Thus by mid-1942, about seven million Jews were under Hitler's control. The question was never whether to murder them, but only what killing method was fast enough and sufficiently cost-effective to accomplish the goal. The Nazis were committed to make the world *Judenrein*—empty of Jews once and for all. In 1939, an office was opened in Berlin for this purpose. In charge was Adolf Eichmann, who was responsible for planning the extermination program. In July 1941, orders were given to "make all preparatory measures required for the final solution of the Jewish question," and the plan for the Final Solution was revealed in January 1942 in Berlin at the Wannsee conference.

While advancing eastward into Russia, special units of the German army, the *Einsatzgruppen,* rounded up the Jews of the conquered towns, herded them into buses or trains, took them to forests or clearings. The Jews were first ordered to dig large pits and afterward the Germans shot them to death, thousands at a time. The victims fell into large pits where their corpses were burned and then covered over. Some 800,000 Russian Jews died this way. In Poland and the Baltic States, Jews from towns and villages were transported into ghettos located in large Polish cities like Warsaw and Lodz. There, many were either starved to death or died of disease. Some 2,000,000 of the 3,300,000 Polish Jews were still alive in March 1942. The extermination rate was too slow, so the Germans built extermination camps throughout Poland and sent the Jews to the camps at a rate of 6,000–10,000 per day. Extermination camps differed from concentration camps. In the latter, Jews were kept and used for labor until they died. In exterminaton camps like Birkenau, they were murdered on arrival, usually by lethal gas. Gas chambers were built disguised as showers. When the Jews arrived at the extermination camps, they were ordered to strip and wash themselves. Once inside the showers, they were gassed and cremated at a rate of 10,000 people each day. By June 1943, only 500,000 Polish Jews remained alive. The Final Solution was reaching its climax: "This is a day of glory in our history which has never been written," proudly announced Himmler to his SS officers.

By February 1944, the last 80,000 Jews of the Lodz ghetto had been sent to Auschwitz for extermination. Some 3,000,000—90 percent—of Polish Jews had been slaughtered; 2,000,000 had been gassed and cremated in Auschwitz alone. Meanwhile, Eichmann was planning a museum in Germany to exhibit an exterminated people and their lost culture. In Western Europe, the extermination rates were not as high, but still reached 75 percent in Holland, and 50 percent in France and Norway. There were heroic stories of righteous European gentiles who saved individual Jews; in Denmark, the king and the Danish people rallied to save the majority of Danish Jews. Yet these remained heroic exceptions to the general rule of complicity and apathy. The Roman Catholic Church protested the Nazi euthanasia program for imbeciles, the genetically deformed, and social undesirables, but neither it nor the German Lutheran Church publicly protested the murder of Jews in their midst.

Historians agree that the most important factor in determining the proportion of Jews exterminated in any country is

Nazi Extermination of European Jews

Country	Estimated Pre-final Solution Population	Estimated Jewish Population Annihilated	Percent
Poland	3,300,000	3,000,000	90
Baltic countries	253,000	228,000	90
Germany/Austria	240,000	210,000	90
Protectorate	90,000	80,000	89
Slovakia	90,000	75,000	83
Greece	70,000	54,000	77
The Netherlands	140,000	105,000	75
Hungary	650,000	450,000	70
SSR White Russia	375,000	245,000	65
SSR Ukraine★	1,500,000	900,000	60
Belgium	65,000	40,000	60
Yugoslavia	43,000	26,000	60
Rumania	600,000	300,000	50
Norway	1,800	900	50
France	350,000	90,000	26
Bulgaria	64,000	14,000	22
Italy	40,000	8,000	20
Luxembourg	5,000	1,000	20
Russia (RFSSR)★	975,000	107,000	11
Denmark	8,000	—	—
Finland	2,000	—	—
Total	**8,861,000**	**5,933,900**	**67**

★The Germans did not occupy all the territory of this republic.

From Lucy Davidowicz, *The War against the Jews* (New York: Holt Reinhart and Winston, 1975), p. 403.

how much the local population assisted with or resisted the Nazis' plans. Without local support, the Final Solution was difficult (though not impossible) to carry out. It is a sobering story indeed that most of Poland, Austria, Russia, and Romania aided the Germans in the killing of the Jews.

When the war ended, two-thirds of Europe's nine million Jews had been murdered. Hundreds of thousands more died shortly after due to malnutrition and disease. After the war, some survivors who tried to return to their home towns, like Kielce in Poland, were killed by the local populations. The continent that 150 years ago promised Jews liberty, equality, and fraternity ended up exterminating the majority of them instead, and in the words of the Bible, "vomited out" the minority that survived. In the end, the Jews of modern Europe were helpless to defend themselves from the slaughter. It proved the biblical claim that exile is a curse—only in terms more tragic and brutal than the Bible could imagine.

If the German Nazis were the main perpetrators of the extermination, the indifference of the allied countries toward European anti-Semitism and Hitler's Final Solution also contributed. When President Roosevelt refused entry to the Jews on the *St. Louis* in 1939, he did not know of the Nazi extermination plan. But world leaders certainly did know by 1943 that millions of Jews were being systematically exterminated in Auschwitz and other camps. Yet even though Allied planes were making bombing runs near the camps, both Churchill and Roosevelt refused Jewish pleas to bomb the railroad tracks that led to Auschwitz in order to stop or at least slow the mass murder of Jews. Near the end of the war while the murder was at its height, the British Near East secretary, Lord Moyne, refused a Nazi offer to trade 100,000 Jews for food and goods, by asking, "What would I do with the Jews?"[27] The sad truth is that no powerful country came to the aid of the Jews who were being hunted down and murdered, even to offer them refuge. The small Jewish community in Palestine, numbering only 200,000 when the genocide began, absorbed more victims of persecution than did the entire United States of America.[28] In Hitler's independent war against the Jews, the Jewish people stood alone, without any allies to rely on.

PART III

RETURNING HOME

Thus said the Lord God: "I will gather you from the peoples and assemble you out of the countries where you have been scattered, and I will give you the Land of Israel."

EZEKIEL 11:17

6

STATEHOOD AND YOUNG ISRAEL

THE JEWISH PROBLEM—AGAIN

FOR ALL INTENTS AND PURPOSES, the Holocaust ended any vibrant Jewish life and culture in Europe. Jewish towns, property, and institutions in Eastern Europe had been destroyed, and all throughout Europe, Jews had been uprooted. Because they had no home after the war, 250,000 Jewish survivors were herded behind barbed wire in displaced-persons (DP) camps in Germany. Going back to Poland or Russia was unthinkable, and England and America refused to increase their immigration quotas. When the United Nations proposed that the small island of Madagascar absorb some displaced persons, that country responded that it would admit some refugees, but "not the city-bred Jews who were worn and emaciated through long confinement in concentration camps."[1] The survivors' predicament was best captured by the poignant lyrics of a Yiddish song of that period:

> Tell me where can I go?
> There's no place I can see,
> Where to go, where to go,
> Every door is closed to me.

> To the left, to the right
> It's the same in every land,
> There is nowhere to go,
> And it's me who should know
> Won't you please understand!

The Jewish refugees themselves knew where they belonged and wanted to go. Here is what Richard Crossman, a British member of Parliament, reported to his government in 1946 after he visited the camps:

> For nine months, huddled together, these Jews had nothing to do but to discuss the future. They knew they were not wanted by the western democracies. They were not Poles any more; but as Hitler had taught them, members of the Jewish nation, despised and rejected by "civilized Europe." They knew that far away in Palestine there was a National Home willing and eager to receive them and to give them a chance of rebuilding their lives, not as aliens in a foreign state but as Hebrews in their own country.[2]

But in 1939, the British had imposed tight restrictions on Jewish immigration to Palestine in their White Paper, and Britain refused to relent even after the Holocaust. The British were fearful of offending oil-rich Arab countries by allowing further Jewish immigration.

Between 1915 and 1939, Jewish immigration to Palestine had risen dramatically and the Jewish population had increased from 85,000 to 448,000. Jews streamed into Palestine from Russia, Poland, Germany, and Romania. It was during this period that Jews founded Tel Aviv and transformed it from a small area on the sand near Jaffa into a city, and established great cultural institutions like the Palestine Symphony Orchestra (later the Israel Philharmonic) in Tel Aviv and the Hebrew University of Jerusalem.

Arabs reacted to the Jews' growing presence and increased political strength by violently attacking Jewish towns and businesses. As a result, in 1920 the Jews of Palestine organized into a body to defend themselves and their property. The clandestine organization was called the Haganah (Hebrew for "defense"), and it was the first time in nearly 2,000 years that Jews were able to take formal responsibility for their own security and defense by use of arms. (The Haganah ultimately became the foundation for the Israel Defense Forces—the Israeli army—when the Jewish State was established in 1948.) As the fighting between Arabs and Jews grew more and more violent, it became evident that Jews and Arabs would each need their own homeland, and that one Jewish-Arab state was not possible. In June 1937, the British Peel Commission recommended partitioning Palestine into a Jewish state and an Arab state. The Jewish leaders of Palestine were disappointed by the small amount of land accorded to the Jewish State, but they accepted this partition compromise. In contrast, the surrounding Arab countries unanimously rejected it and any other compromise, insisting that "Britain had to choose between our friendship and the Jews."[3]

The Jewish leadership believed that Palestine could absorb a large number of Jews and Arabs. Most of the land was still undeveloped, and there was no need for Jews to displace any Arabs. The Arabs refused to recognize this, and because they refused to allow even a small area of Palestine to be ruled by Jews, they intensified their attacks.

When the situation inside Palestine became critical in 1939, England abandoned the partition plan and reneged on its earlier basic policy of allowing Jewish immigration until part of Palestine had a Jewish majority. So at the very time that the Nazis were imposing racial laws against the Jews in

Europe, Britain passed the White Paper restricting the total Jewish immigration from 1939 to 1944 to 100,000. By 1945, 553,000 Jews were living in Palestine. Although England had closed the gates to Jewish immigration, Jews were determined to come to their homeland. From 1945 to 1947, another 40,000 Jews arrived illegally on small ships under the darkness of night. Not all managed to set foot in Palestine. The British caught more than 51,000 Jewish refugees from the displaced-persons camps of Europe trying to get to Palestine and quarantined them behind barbed wire in DP camps in Cyprus. Others, like the passengers on the small ship the *Exodus*, heroically went on a hunger strike after being caught by the British. When the world saw that the Jews of the *Exodus* would rather die than be denied entry to their homeland, the British were embarrassed into allowing them into Palestine.

In 1946 the American-Anglo Commission on Palestine recommended to Britain that 100,000 Jews in the DP camps be allowed to enter Palestine immediately to alleviate their great suffering, yet Britain still refused to allow further immigration. Palestinian Jews began to see the British as an enemy that was training and even arming the Arabs, and responded by establishing more new Jewish towns and striking against British installations in Palestine. An undeclared war began between Palestinian Jews and the British. A small group of dissenting Jews broke from Haganah policy, formed the Irgun (Organization), and began to engage in terror operations against British soldiers and officials. The Haganah condemned this terrorist fringe and took action against it. Meanwhile, the highest Arab religious leader in Palestine, the grand mufti of Jerusalem, who had lived in Berlin during World War II, directed the Arabs to escalate terrorism against Jewish civilians. Attacks against Jewish towns increased, and Palestine descended into chaos between 1946 and 1947.

It was obvious that England could not govern Palestine, and Britain handed the problem of Palestine over to the United Nations in February 1947. Dr. Chaim Weizmann made the following plea for a Jewish homeland to the UN Special Committee on Palestine:

> What are the Poles? What are the French? What are the Swiss? When that is asked, everyone points to a country, to parliamentary institutions, and the man on the street knows exactly what it is. He has a passport.
>
> If you ask what a Jew is—well, he is a man who has to offer a long explanation for his existence, and any person who has to offer an explanation as to what he is, is always suspect—and from suspicion there is only one step to hatred or contempt.
>
> Why Palestine? Why not Alaska or Kamchatka? It was the responsibility of Moses, who acted from divine inspiration. He could have brought us to the United States, and instead of the Jordan we would have the Mississippi. But he chose to stop here. We are an ancient people with an old history. You cannot deny your history and begin afresh.[4]

THE BIRTH OF ISRAEL

The UN commission recommended partitioning Palestine into Jewish and Arab states, as Britain had done ten years earlier. Once again, the Arab leaders rejected this compromise proposal. The Jewish leadership, known as the Jewish Agency, accepted the compromise even though the plan kept a quarter of Palestine's Jews outside the area of Jewish statehood. On November 29, 1947, the UN General Assembly voted to accept the partition plan by a vote of 33–13. The United

States, the Soviet Union, Canada, France, and Holland voted for the proposal. The Soviet Union UN representative, Andrey Gromyko, stated:

> The decision to partition Palestine is in keeping with the high principles and aims of the United Nations. It is in keeping with the principle of the national self-determination of peoples.... The solution of the Palestine problem based on a partition of Palestine into two separate states will be of profound historical significance, because this decision will meet the legitimate demands of the Jewish people, hundreds of thousands of whom, as you know, are still without a country, without homes, having found temporary shelter only in special camps in some western European countries.[5]

The partition plan also recommended that Jewish immigration be reopened in early 1948. At long last, the Holocaust survivors would be able to come home.

Jews all around the world rejoiced when the UN voted to create the Jewish state, but there was also great fear. All six Arab member states of the UN had voted against the partition plan, and the surrounding Arab countries declared their intention to invade Palestine as soon as the British evacuated. The mufti of Jerusalem, an ally of Hitler, made no secret of Arab genocidal intentions. He declared a holy war and urged his brother Muslims to slaughter the Jews, while the leaders of surrounding Arab countries threatened to destroy the new country and "throw the Jews into the sea." Jews understood that they faced a war with the odds overwhelmingly against them. This time, however, they would have the opportunity to defend their lives, their freedom, and their right to self-determination.

The British forces evacuated on May 14, 1948, and on that very afternoon, David Ben-Gurion declared the establishment of the first independent Jewish state in almost 2,000 years—the State of Israel. Jews all around the world were filled with pride and hope. American Supreme Court justice Felix Frankfurter wrote to Chaim Weizmann: "Mine eyes have seen the coming of the glory of the Lord; happily you can now say that, and can say what Moses could not."[6] (Moses was never able to enter the Promised Land. Deuteronomy 34 indicates that he died on Mt. Nebo near the eastern bank of the Jordan River.) The leaders of Israel proclaimed that every Jew would have a right to citizenship in the Jewish State; no Jew would ever again have to suffer persecution because there was no place that would accept and protect him or her. Israel would also be a home to Jews everywhere, where the Jewish people could build its own culture and values in freedom and independence.

Although the majority of those modern Zionists were not religious Jews, they understood that the only place where Jews could be free was in their biblical homeland, which was the cradle of Jewish culture and civilization. In establishing a pluralistic democracy, they were faithful to the covenantal dream and its ideals of peace and justice as stated in the Bible: "You shall proclaim liberty throughout the land for all its inhabitants" (Leviticus 25:10). Even more, Israel must be a place of freedom and justice for all people—not only Jews. These ideals were inscribed in Israel's Declaration of Independence:

> The State of Israel will be open for Jewish immigration and for the Ingathering of the Exiles; it will foster the development of the country for the benefit of all its inhabitants; it will be based on freedom, justice and peace as envisaged by the prophets of Israel; it will ensure complete equality of social and political rights to all its

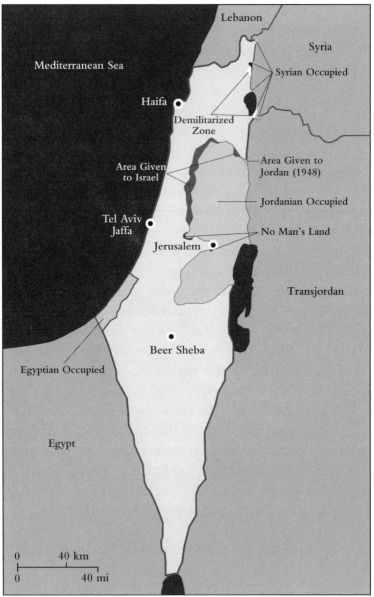

Mediterranean Sea

Lebanon

Syria

Syrian Occupied

Haifa

Demilitarized
Zone

Area Given
to Israel

Area Given to
Jordan (1948)

Jordanian Occupied

Tel Aviv
Jaffa

No Man's Land

Jerusalem

Transjordan

Beer Sheba

Egyptian Occupied

Egypt

0   40 km

0   40 mi

1949–1967 Armistice Lines

ive of religion, race or sex; it will

f religion, conscience, language, edu-

will safeguard the Holy Places of all

be faithful to the principles of the

d Nations....

hand to all neighbouring states and

offer of peace and good neighbourli-

em to establish bonds of cooperation

h the sovereign Jewish people settled

e State of Israel is prepared to do its

effort for the advancement of the

el was established, there were approximately 657,000 Jews living there. On the very day that independence was declared, Egyptian aircraft bombed Tel Aviv, the largest Jewish city, and Iraqi troops crossed the Jordan River. A total of five Arab countries crossed into Palestine from every direction. Although badly outnumbered and outgunned, small Israel was prepared. For the tiny country and its new citizens, the choice was stark: victory or death.

The War of Independence lasted from May 1948 until January 1949. Somehow, Israel managed to defeat the invading Arab enemies, but the cost was enormous. About 6,000 Israelis—nearly 1 out of every 100—lost their lives in the struggle. (By comparison, if America had lost the same percentage in World War II, approximately 1.4 million Americans would have died.) On February 24, Egypt and Israel signed an armistice agreement under UN auspices. In March, Israel signed cease-fire agreements with Jordan and Iraq. Israel wanted to sign peace agreements to permanently end all hostilities with her neighbors and usher in a period of cooperation, but the Arab countries insisted on cease-fire agreements alone. Peace agreements would imply recognition, and even in defeat the Arab countries adamantly refused to recognize that Israel had a rightful place in the Middle East. Rather than create an Arab state for Palestinian Arabs as the partition plan had recommended, Jordan occupied the area immediately west of the Jordan River and annexed it as part of Transjordan.

One condition of the armistice agreement with Jordan specified that Israelis were allowed access to Jerusalem's holy sites in the ancient part of the city, and to Mount Scopus, where Jews had built the Hebrew University and Hadassah Hospital and which remained Israeli sovereign territory. But Jordan reneged on this commitment, and Jerusalem was divided between the Israeli side on the west and the Jordanian-occupied side on the east. Jews were not allowed to enter the Old City of Jerusalem to pray at the Western Wall or to visit the Temple Mount or other holy sites there, nor were they allowed access to Hadassah Hospital and Hebrew University on Mt. Scopus. Although the Jordanians allowed Christians to go from West Jerusalem to the Old City, the closest Jews could get to the Western Wall was a view of the ancient city's exterior walls through binoculars from behind the barbed wire that separated Jewish Jerusalem from the part of the city occupied by the Jordanians.

Despite these disappointments, the Jewish people had risen from the ashes of Auschwitz to build a vibrant homeland with its own language, flag, army, government, and anthem, "Hatikvah," "The Hope." The words of the anthem convey the love and longing that the Jewish people have long had for their homeland:

> As long as in the heart, within,
> A Jewish soul is yearning,
> And to the edges of the East, eastward,
> An eye watches towards Zion,

Our hope is not yet lost,
The hope of two thousand years
To be a free nation in our own land,
The land of Zion and Jerusalem.

Jews hoped that at long last they would be able to create a free
and secure national life in their own homeland. Like the
famous dry bones described by the prophet Ezekiel, the Jewish
people had again come to life in their ancient land:

> "I will put My breath into you and you shall live again. I
> will set you upon you soil," declares the Lord. "Thus they
> shall remain in the land which I gave to My servant Jacob
> and in which your fathers dwelt, they and their children
> and their children's children.... I will make a covenant of
> friendship with them—It shall be an everlasting covenant
> with them." (Ezekiel 37:14, 25–26)

THE INGATHERING OF THE EXILES

After the cease fire ended the War of Independence, Jews from
around the world began to stream into the new State of Israel.
The Israeli population doubled in three years, and by 1957 it
had tripled. More than 800,000 Jews were driven out of their
homes in Egypt, Morocco, Iraq, Iran, Yemen, Syria, Tunisia,
and Libya due to increased Muslim hostility against them after
Israel won the war.[7] More than 600,000 of these refugees
found their way to Israel, which absorbed them, gave them
new homes, and made them proud citizens of their own country. Thousands more Jews immigrated or made *aliyah* to Israel
from France, Germany, Hungary, and America. This *aliyah*
echoed the 2,500-year-old words of Deuteronomy, Isaiah,
Jeremiah, and Ezekiel[8] that Jews scattered throughout the

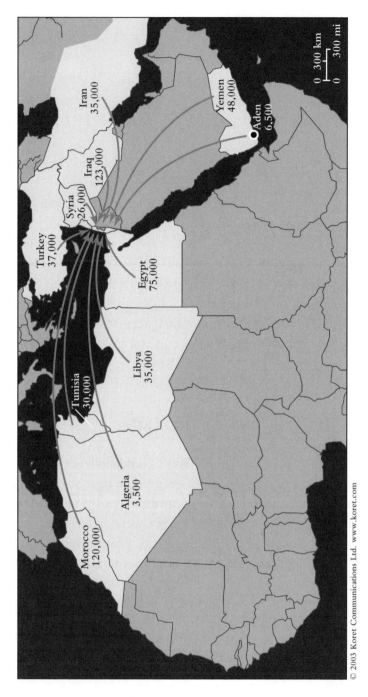

Refugees to Israel from Muslim Countries

Diaspora would be gathered from the four corners of the earth and return home to the land of Israel.

Over the next fourteen years, more than 1,500,000 Jews would come to Israel to begin new lives and join the Jewish people there. By 1964, the Jewish population of Israel had grown to 2,100,000. Because of tremendous economic and scientific development, continuing immigration, and natural growth, Israel now has 7,150,000 citizens, of whom 5,725,000 are Jewish, while 1,425,000 are Muslim and Christian.

The State of Israel has had an enormously powerful effect on Jews in the Diaspora to this day. It touches their emotions and identity to the core, and has transformed them into proud Jews who admire the heroism and accomplishments of the Jewish State in the face of enemies who still want to destroy it. During World War II, American Jews were too insecure and timid to ask the American government to help save the Jews of Europe. The dignity that Israel has given them has helped them become more confident to organize politically and to effectively represent themselves and the Jewish people. Israel has had similar effects on the millions of Jewish people in Russia. On the Jewish New Year holiday, Rosh Hashanah, in 1949, less than nine months after Israel ended its War of Independence, 50,000 Jews packed into the main synagogue of Moscow to greet Israel's first ambassador to Russia, Golda Meir, and to express their profound desire to participate in the miracle of the establishment of the Jewish State.[9] "Next year in Jerusalem," they shouted. They were then forbidden by Russia to emigrate. In the 1950s Soviet Jews suffered from Stalin's anti-Semitic policies and were persecuted by the athiest Communist regime for practicing Judaism, expressing Jewish identity, and advocating for human rights. Eventually they won the right to emigrate, and more than 1,000,000 Soviet Jews came to Israel to make the Jewish State their new home.

EARLY CHALLENGES

In addition to absorbing the flood of Jews from around the world and defending Israel against her neighbors, the new country was incredibly successful in building the essential institutions of statehood. Because Jews had learned the harsh lessons of dictatorship and exclusion, the Israelis established a parliamentary democracy, with the Knesset of 120 elected officials as its legislative body. Israel's executive branch consisted of a coalition of parties representing a variety of political positions, and its first prime minister was David Ben-Gurion. Israel convened a Supreme Court of judicial experts and established a legal system built on the existing Anglo-Saxon law from the British mandate period, as well as elements of Turkish law and classic Jewish law. It left the writing of a constitution for a later period, but succeeded in constructing a liberal Western society where all citizens have a voice and a vote—the first such society in the Middle East. The government also established lower courts, started a diplomatic corps, welfare services, labor unions, schools and educational centers, and a housing administration. Israel's citizens in the early years were characterized by an indomitable will to live, rich native intelligence, and skills acquired from years in exile. This continues up until today. The country became incredibly vibrant after statehood, and this vitality continues to energize Israeli culture today.

Building the new country required huge sums of money. Israeli taxes soon became the highest in the world but were still unable to cover government costs. Moreover, the Arabs maintained a tight boycott that closed off Israel's natural markets, and foreign investors were hesitant to put money into the vulnerable war-torn country. The early 1950s were times of great economic and personal difficulty. Israelis lived poorly, and they were so short of money and goods that men were often forced to wear shorts because long pants requiring more fabric were considered a luxury. In 1951, Ben Gurion came to America to raise money for bonds for Israel. American Jews responded spontaneously and generously, purchasing $250,000,000 in Israel bonds. Together with German reparations, this money helped Israel stem inflation and become economically stable.

Throughout the early years, Israelis gradually made scientific and agriculture breakthroughs. They discovered new techniques to purify salt water and sewage, and rechanneled pure water around the country. The pre-State pioneering spirit endured after statehood, and Israelis drained the swamps of the north and made the Negev desert in the south bloom. By 1955, Israel had irrigated four times as much land as had been irrigated in 1948. By 1957, Israeli scientists had built a nuclear reactor to provide energy, as Israel is poor in oil and other natural energy resources.

Israeli society posed daunting social challenges. Jews came from dozens of countries and cultures. Along with scientists from Europe and America were Jews from Arab countries that had never experienced the industrial revolution, or modern enlightenment. Could all these Jews live together, learn to understand one another, and become part of one unified national culture? The educational and social obstacles were almost insurmountable. Meanwhile, 160,000 Arabs chose to stay in Israel after the War of Independence. They were full citizens like all others, but wanted to live a different culture in separate communities, and the Israeli government was responsible for their social and economic welfare.

Through all the social and economic challenges, Israeli culture flourished. In 1953–1954, Israelis succeeded in publishing 1,000 scholarly and popular articles—or ten times the per capita amount that was published in America. There was an extraordinary diversity of cultural expression. During this period, Arab terrorism and military hostility did not let up. In 1956, Egypt closed off international waterways to Israeli shipping—an act of war according to international law. Israel was forced to go to war and occupy the Sinai desert to defend herself. After opening up the waterways and withdrawing to the prewar lines, President Gamal Abdul Nasser of Egypt repeated the same threat by closing the Straits of Tiran and pulling the Egyptian army up to the Israeli border in May and June of 1967. War broke out then and again in 1973, when Arab armies again invaded (see chapter 8).

Despite the unparalleled and unceasing military burden, the spirit, energy, and talent of the Israelis allowed the young country to reach political, economic, scientific, and cultural heights. Israel consolidated its place in the family of nations and became the center of Jewish national culture for Jewish life everywhere. In addition to its role as a safe haven offering security to Jews, Israel was significant in its role as the place where Jews could attempt a renaissance of the ethical grandeur of the Bible and the Hebrew prophets. Here is how Israel's first president, Chaim Weizmann, put it in his autobiography:

> Whether prophets will once more arise among the Jews is difficult to say. But if they choose the way of honest and hard and clean living on the land in settlements built on old principles; if they center their activities on genuine values, whether in industry, agriculture, science, literature or art, then God will look down benignly on His children who after a long wandering have come home to serve Him with a psalm on their lips and a spade in their hands, reviving an old country and making it a center of human civilization.[10]

7

ISRAEL TODAY

AS THE ONLY DEMOCRACY in the Middle East, modern Israel is a dynamic country. It is a pluralistic society that guarantees freedom of religion and equality under the law for all of its citizens. It has become the center of Jewish life for Jews around the world and the fountain of contemporary Jewish culture. Because of its prominence in world affairs and Jewish culture, Israel is the public face of the Jewish people today.

By 2020, more Jews will live in Israel than in the Diaspora. Israel has transformed Jews from being vulnerable and persecuted wanderers without roots into a strong and vibrant nation that has returned to natural history. Like all peoples, the Jewish people is now connected to geography and it struggles with the real-life challenges of politics, economics, self-defense, immigration and emigration, social justice, and diplomacy. Israel has diplomatic relations with the majority of countries in the world and is a member of the United Nations. In short, the State of Israel has enabled the Jewish people to take its place among the nations of the earth, and bestowed upon Jews the blessings of self-determination and the freedom to develop their own values and culture. The developing culture of Israel is the most important element in shaping the future of the Jewish people and Judaism. In the prophetic words of Isaiah, "From Zion will come Torah and the word of God from Jerusalem."

Ethiopian Jews of Israel

THE PEOPLE OF ISRAEL

Israeli society has developed into a rich, colorful tapestry. Although it is the Jewish homeland, its people are religiously, ethnically, and culturally diverse. In 2006, its total population was 7,100,000 people, with 5,600,000 Jews, 1,200,000 Muslims and Christians, and 300,000 Druze and Bedouin.[1]

In many ways, modern Israel has fulfilled the biblical promise of ingathering the exiles. The more than one million Russian-Jewish refugees who came to Israel fleeing oppression and discrimination are now contributing to nearly every aspect of Israeli life, particularly in music, science, academics, and athletics.

More than 50,000 Ethiopian Jews are citizens of Israel today. They believe they are the descendants of King Solomon and the Queen of Sheba. In the 1980s and 1990s, the Israeli government mass-airlifted them into Israel. This is the only instance in the twentieth century of a non-African country voluntarily encouraging and accepting a large number of black Africans for citizenship. The Ethiopian Jews grew up in a primitive agricultural culture, and integrating them into a modern scientific society has presented Israel with enormous social and educational challenges. Nevertheless, these Ethiopians are gradually adapting and progressing in Israeli life. Many are now leaders and officers in the Israeli army, and others are active in social and educational institutions throughout Israel.

The majority of Israeli Jews are "Sephardim"—Jews whose families came recently from Muslim lands and cultures. Most of those immigrants came from pre-industrial societies in Yemen, Iraq, Morocco, Libya, and Egypt. Israel introduced them to democratic and scientific culture and successfully educated them for leadership in the modern world. Many Israeli presidents, chiefs of staff, generals, cabinet ministers, and parliament members have been Sephardic Jews. A large minority of

Israeli Jews are "Ashkenazim"—Jews who came from Christian countries in western, central and eastern Europe. As the original leaders of modern Zionism, they were in the forefront of building and leading young Israel. Today, however, there is a greater balance between Ashkenazic and Sephardic leadership in the country. Israel's success in integrating millions of Jews from so many diverse cultural, racial, and educational backgrounds into one national entity is truly astounding.

Since Israel was established, Arab Israeli citizens have undergone positive changes that are unparalleled in any other Muslim or Arab community in the world—all despite the continuing war between Israel and her Arab neighbors. The Israeli Arab population has increased from the 160,000 who chose not to flee Israel before the War of Independence to more than one million today. Israel's Arabs have chosen to "vote with their feet," and Arab emigration out of Israel is almost nonexistent. Arabic is one of Israel's two official languages; Arabs belong to mainstream political parties, and some have formed their own official Arab parties. Arabs are members of the Knesset and the diplomatic corps, and they sit on the Israeli Supreme Court.

Arabs are guaranteed legal equality, but they have not yet attained social or economic equality. Israel is an imperfect democracy, and illegal discrimination exists. Although Arabs have a lower per capita income than Israeli Jews, the economic status of Israeli Arabs is similar to that of other Israelis who have large families with only one wage earner.[2] Only 13 percent of Israeli Muslim women choose to work outside the home, compared to 52 percent of Israeli Jewish women. In addition, the economic disparity between Jews and Arabs in Israel is less than the disparities between non-Arabs and Arabs in other democracies like France, Germany, England, and the United States.[3]

Israeli Arabs are better educated and healthier than their Arab neighbors. The average number of years of education for

Israel's Arabs is 11.2, close to the 12.6 years for Israel's non-Arabs—and the gap is closing. At the University of Haifa, 20 percent of the student body and 10 percent of the faculty is Arab. The Arab illiteracy rate in Israel is only 6 percent, while in Jordan, it is 10 percent; in Lebanon, 13.5 percent; in Syria 20.4 percent; and in Egypt, it is 28.6 percent. Similarly, Israeli Arabs have a longer life expectancy (76 years) than do Arabs in Syria (73 years), Lebanon (72 years), Jordan (71 years), and Egypt (less than 70 years). Israel's Arabs also have a significantly lower infant mortality rate than do their Arab neighbors. It is obvious why almost no Israeli Arabs leave Israel for Arab countries or even Europe.

CHRISTIANS IN ISRAEL

Israel's Christians are in a uniquely privileged situation in the Middle East. While there is a general Christian exodus out of Muslim countries in the Middle East, Israel remains the only country in the region where the number of Christians has grown in the last sixty years. In 1948, Israel was home to approximately 34,000 Christians, yet today there are between 130,000 and 140,000 Christian Israeli citizens. In Jerusalem, the number of Christians decreased from 18,000 in 1948 to 10,000 in 1967, when the city was under Jordanian control. Under the Israelis, the Christian population has rebounded to about 15,000 today. The majority of Israeli Christians are Greek Orthodox, but Catholics, Protestants, and Russian Orthodox also live in Israel. Christians flourish because Israel is a democracy that guarantees freedom of religion and protects minority rights.

In this time of rising Islamic nationalism throughout the Middle East, Christians throughout the region and in the Palestinian-controlled territories are experiencing acute harassment and oppression.[4] Conversion to Christianity is punishable by death under Palestinian law. Bethlehem was 80 percent Christian in 1995 when Israel gave administrative control of the city to the Palestinian Authority. Today, Bethlehem is less than 20 percent Christian; Christian businesses have been forced to close, and Christians are being driven out. Ramallah was once a Christian town, but hardly any Christians are left because it has become the center for Palestinian and Islamic political activity. In contrast to the increase in the Israeli Christian populations, most Christians who have enough money are fleeing the Palestinian territories.[5]

THE LAND AND ITS SITES

Israel is a narrow country, about 290 miles long and 85 miles wide at its greatest point (see map, p. 92). Although small, it has a dazzling array of landscapes, natural wonders, and famous places. Mountains, plains, and deserts are often just minutes away from one another. The Galilee region in the north is lush and verdant, filled with mountains, valleys, and the famous Sea of Galilee that is so prominent in Christian scripture and history. A bit to the south is the narrow coastal plain where more than half of all Israelis live. (This dense concentration in such a small area makes the population strategically vulnerable.) The plain has a beautiful, eighty-mile-long Mediterranean coast, the major cities of Tel Aviv and Haifa, deep-water harbors, and fertile agricultural fields. In the center of the country is Israel's capital, the holy city of Jerusalem, situated in the Judean hills and on the edge of the Judean desert. In the south is the now-modern biblical city of Be'er Sheva, where today a tourist can see camel herds grazing next to modern hospitals and universities. The southernmost third of Israel is the Negev desert, which Israeli science and ingenuity has helped to make bloom.

At the southern tip of the country is the tourist haven of Eilat, with lavish hotels on the crystal-clear waters of the Red Sea. The famous Jordan River runs north-south to the east, from the Sea of Galilee to the Dead Sea—the lowest point on earth. The country is a dynamic mixture of the old and the new, the biblical and the modern, attracting more than two millions tourists each year from all over the world.

The Land and its sites bedazzle natives and tourists alike, bringing the Bible, history, and religious identity to life. A favorite recreational activity of Israelis is touring the length and breadth of the country during the holidays and summer months. On these days, the Galilee is filled with Jews picnicking around the Sea of Galilee and in the city of Tsefat, where Jewish mystics once flourished, and visiting nearby Tiberias, where Talmudic Rabbis presided and where the tomb of the great medieval Rabbi and philosopher Maimonides is located. Throngs of people come to Jerusalem to the site of the First and Second Temples, the archaeological excavations that reveal Jewish life during the Temple times, the purported tomb of King David, and the location of his original city of Jerusalem.

Slightly to the south, Israel's citizens and tourists flock to the biblical matriarch Rachel's tomb outside Bethlehem; to Masada, where Jews fought off the Roman armies before committing suicide in 73 CE; and to Herodium to view Herod's palace and his recently discovered tomb. Other favorite spots are the Jerusalem Biblical Zoo and the park at Ne'ot Kedumim, where biblical flora and fauna are lovingly cultivated and exhibited. One of the most popular organizations is the Society for the Protection of Nature in Israel (Hachevrah Lahaganat Hateva), which organizes tours throughout Israel's parks, lakes, mountains, and deserts. All this contrasts with the discos, opera, cafes, and night life of the ultramodern city of Tel Aviv—the "City That Never Sleeps."

Christians also celebrate the Land and Israel's religious sites. On Christmas, special services are held at the Church of the Nativity in Bethlehem, where Jesus was born, and at the Church of the Annunciation in Nazareth, where Jesus grew up. Particularly during Holy Week, Christians from all around the world visit Jerusalem. On Easter, pilgrims march through the Via Dolorosa, stopping at the Stations of the Cross, and pray at the Church of the Holy Sepulchre where Jesus was crucified. Year round, Christians visit the Sea of Galilee and the nearby Mount of the Beatitudes, where Jesus delivered the Sermon on the Mount, as well as the synagogue at Capernaum where Jesus preached. The Christian community of Nes Ammim lives throughout the year in the Galilee to draw inspiration from the Land and people of Jesus' life. Finally, the port city of Haifa functions as the world headquarters of the Baha'i faith, which was considered heretic by Muslim clerics and whose worshippers were driven out of Arab lands in the Middle East.

JERUSALEM

Both the spiritual and political capital of Israel, Jerusalem exercises a unique hold on Jews beyond any other place in Israel. Jewish liturgy is filled with prayers for the welfare and restoration of the city. According to Jewish law and tradition, Jerusalem is endowed with special holiness. For religious Jews, Jerusalem's Temple Mount still possesses so much holiness that Jews are forbidden to walk on it, for fear that they might trample on the site of the Temple's Holy of Holies. Religious and Talmudic academies abound in Jerusalem, and religious Jews consider living in the holy city a special blessing. Throughout its 3,000-year history, the city has been conquered by the Babylonians, Romans, Byzantines, Crusaders, Egyptian Ayyubids and Mamluks, Ottomans, and Jordanians. Yet only the ancient Jews, the twelfth-century Crusaders, and the Jewish people of today considered Jerusalem important enough to make it their capital. (Jerusalem was the religious capital for the Crusaders only because Crusader kings and officials governed from the northern city of Acre.) Only today under Jewish rule is there complete and guaranteed freedom of religion to all the city's residents.

Because of its special religious value to both Jews and Christians, Jerusalem is the home of the Israeli chief rabbinate and the Greek and Latin church patriarchs. On Jewish holidays, the city is filled with religious and nonreligious Jews who come to witness public rituals and experience spiritual moments. On Easter and Christmas, a great number of Christian pilgrims celebrate the holidays in the very places in the city where Jesus often walked. Jerusalem is also home to Israel's national institutions and political leaders—the Knesset, the Israeli Supreme Court, and the residences of both the prime minister and the president.

Today, Jerusalem is a large city of more than 725,000 residents, approximately two-thirds Jewish and one-third Arab. It grew from an undeveloped and undesirable town under Ottoman rule into a small city under British rule between the World Wars into a bustling modern metropolis under Israeli sovereignty. Jerusalem mixes the old and the modern, the holy and the mundane. Ancient Jewish, Christian, and Muslim holy sites are located inside the Old City walls, while modern malls, industrial parks, universities, and stadiums flank the north and south of the city.

As mentioned in chapter 6, after Jordan conquered the eastern part of the city in 1948, the Jordanians divided Jerusalem with barbed wire and fences. In violation of the armistice agreement, Jordan prevented Jews from visiting Jewish holy sites and Mount Scopus in the eastern sector. Jordanian army snipers often fired from rooftop positions on Jewish residents in the western part of the city. The bullet-ridden stones and physical evidence of that division remain even today. After the Six-Day War, the Israelis tore down the barbed wire and passageways, thus unifying the city. Jews were again able to live in the Old City's Jewish Quarter, from which they had been evicted in 1948. Israel restored the area around the Western Wall so that Jews could again pray at their holiest site. Even though Israel now has sovereignty over all Jerusalem, in the interest of political stability, it granted the Muslim Waqf administrative control over the Temple Mount because the Al-Aqsa Mosque and the Dome of the Rock are located there. Muslims pray at those sites, but it is difficult for Jews to gain access to the Temple Mount for prayer or other purposes.

When Israel unified Jerusalem, it extended Israeli citizenship to all Arab residents of the city. Many refused to become Israeli citizens, but Israel has still granted them access to medical and social services. Because of the special love that Jews have for Jerusalem and its unique religious and historical significance, Israel formally ratified the Jerusalem Covenant in 2002, on the twenty-fifth anniversary of the city's unification. The covenant expresses the profound attachment of the Jewish people for the city and the resolve to maintain sovereignty over it. The president of Israel declared at the signing, "Jerusalem is our one and eternal capital. It will never again endure foreign rule." Then mayor of Jerusalem (and future prime minister) Ehud Olmert said, "Jerusalem is a city open to all religions and will remain open to the faithful of all religions. For three thousand years Jerusalem was the capital of no other nation but ours, and it never will be."[6]

This is the will of the Jewish people—religious and secular alike. This profound conviction is a modern expression of the ancient biblical hope of King David in Psalm 122:

I rejoiced when they said to me,
"We are going to the house of the Lord."
Our feet stood inside your gates, O Jerusalem,
Jerusalem built up, a city knit together,
to which tribes will make pilgrimage,
the tribes of the Lord
—as was enjoined upon Israel—
to praise the name of the Lord.
Pray for the well-being of Jerusalem;
May those who love you be at peace. May there be well-
    being within your ramparts,
peace in your citadels."

GOVERNMENT AND LAW

Israel is a liberal Western democracy in which the government is determined by elections and leaders are continually account-able to the country's citizens. It is the only country in the Middle East where multiple political parties present real choices between candidates, and elections are competitive. (Elections in Egypt, Syria, and Jordan are formalities where one candidate usually receives between 95 and 100 percent of the votes.) The government consists of the legislative branch (the Knesset), the executive branch (cabinet ministers), the judiciary (Israeli supreme court), and the presidency, which is primarily a ceremonial office. The government is led by the prime minister, who is the leader of the party gaining the most popular votes. Parliamentary elections are scheduled every four years, or earlier if the governing coalition calls for them. Like the United States, Israel's system is based on the separation of powers, and the independence of the courts is guaranteed by law. This makes Israel a society where the rule of law is strong, in contrast to many Middle East countries where royal power and arbitrary one-person rule determine how the society is governed.

Although it is a Jewish state, Israel has consciously limited the political power of its ecclesiastical leaders. Rabbis, church leaders, and imams have authority over the personal status of individuals (such as marriage, divorce, and conversion) in their respective communities, but they do not exercise governmental power outside this limited area. There is no absolute separation of church and state in Israel, but as a liberal democracy, Israel bears no resemblance to a theocracy ruled by religious authorities.

Like all thriving democracies, new laws and government actions are subject to judicial review to ensure that they are consistent with the fundamental legal principles of the state and do not violate civil and human rights. The Knesset has enacted a series of basic laws relating to all aspects of life. The Basic Law, entitled Human Dignity and Liberty, ensures there is no violation of the life, body, property, privacy, dignity, and freedom of any citizen and also guarantees the rights of free entry and exit from Israel. Another basic law is called Freedom of Occupation, which guarantees the right to engage in the occupation or trade of one's choosing. Both these laws explicitly state that "fundamental human rights in Israel are founded upon the recognition of the value of the human being, the sanctity of human life, and the principle that all persons are free."[7] Israel's Knesset is now at work writing a constitution, and for now, these basic laws serve as Israel's Bill of Rights.

As have all countries in time of war, Israel has been forced to balance its fundamental commitment to human rights with the need to protect its citizens against terror and attack. Israel's dedication to law and justice means that it extends rights of petition even to noncitizen Palestinians living outside the country on the West Bank:

One of the most unusual aspects of Israeli law is the rapid access that petitioners, including Palestinians, can gain to Israel's highest court. In April 2002, during the fiercest fighting of the current conflict … the high court was receiving and ruling on petitions almost daily.[8]

Though forced to be in a constant state of military readiness and active self-defense against its enemies, Israel has created a flourishing pluralistic democracy dedicated to equal human and civil rights for all its citizens including Arabs, minorities, and women. Israel has struggled to remain true to its original dream and announced in its 1948 Declaration of Independence: "[Israel] will be based on freedom, justice and peace.… [I]t will ensure complete equality of social and political rights … irrespective of religion, race or sex; it will guarantee freedom of religion, conscience, language, education and culture; it will safeguard the Holy Places of all religions.[9]

Education, Science, and Technology

As the Bible (Deuteronomy 11:10–12) indicates, Israel is a land that is short of water. It has almost no oil and lacks plentiful natural resources. Its most valuable resources are its people and their talents. Israel knows that the key to building a responsible national and democratic multiethnic culture is effective education that imparts a love of tradition, of the Land of Israel, of scientific and technological development, and of the principles of liberty and tolerance. Israel has dedicated itself to education for all its citizens and become famous for its world-class research and contributions to nearly every field of human culture.

Israel spends almost 10 percent of its gross domestic product on education. Pre-university education is free and compulsory for all Israeli children from ages five to sixteen. Israel's children attend school for more years than in any other country in the region, and its citizens have the highest literacy rate in the Middle East. Because different religious and ethnic communities want some say in the education their children receive, the public educational system has three separate tracks; one for nonreligious Jews, one for religious Jews, and one for Arabs. In these schools, children from Ethiopia, Russia, Morocco, Yemen, India, Europe, and North and South America become modern Israelis.

In the field of higher education, Israel boasts seven universities and additional research centers that are among the best in the world. It has the world's highest per capita rate of university degrees. The Weizmann Institute of Science in Rehovot is one of the world's leading institutions for scientific research, and the Technion in Haifa has built an international reputation for excellence in applied scientific research and engineering.

The results of Israel's higher education are astounding: Israel has the world's highest ratio of scientists and technicians in the workforce, and Israel produces more scientific papers per capita than any other country in the world. It also has the second highest per capita output of new books. Israel ranks third in the world in per capita patents, behind only the United States and Japan, and has the world's third highest rate of entrepreneurs—and the highest rate for women.[10] Israel has produced eight Nobel laureates in the fields of literature, economics, chemistry, and peace.

Although the number of its people is negligible in the world population, Israel has become a powerful force in global technological and economic development, and a major contributor to medical research around the world. It has its own Silicon Valley, and in the 1990s it became the world's fourth largest high-tech economy. Global giants like Microsoft, Intel, and IBM have built large research and development (R&D) centers in Israel, and these companies rely on Israeli ingenuity for their products. Israeli researchers developed the Motorola cell phone, most of the Windows NT operating system, AOL Instant Messaging, voice-mail technology, the first PC antivirus software, and nanotechnology. Israelis also developed Intel's Pentium 4 microprocessor for desktop computers and the Centrino processor for laptops. Today it is impossible to use a telephone or a computer without using some technology developed in Israel. It is also a world R&D leader in robotics, aeronautics, solar and thermal energy, drip irrigation, optics, and lasers. After the United States and Canada, Israel has the most companies listed on the NASDAQ exchange.

Israel also has an extensive system of world-class medical services and is a world leader in medical and biological research. Health services in Israel are universal for its citizens, partially socialized, and relatively inexpensive. The services are the highest quality in the Middle East, and Israel has performed surgical procedures on Arab royal-family members who could not receive those services in their own countries. Hadassah Hospital in Jerusalem is known throughout the world for its trauma and research centers, and Ichilov Hospital in Tel Aviv has a world-renowned neurosurgery center. Israel is among the world's leaders in research in human reproduction and in vitro fertilization techniques and services. Israeli biomedical companies have developed vaccines that are used throughout the world to treat anthrax, as well as groundbreaking treatments or cures for diabetes and Alzheimer's disease, and safe imaging techniques to diagnose breast cancer. The Israeli pharmaceutical company Teva has grown to become the largest generic drug company in the world and developed a drug to treat Parkinson's disease that is used on a worldwide basis.

ISRAEL'S COMMITMENT TO HUMANITARIAN ASSISTANCE

Because of the long history of Jewish refugees fleeing persecution and of terrorist attacks against Israelis, Israel understands the suffering of dispossessed people and victims of violence. Moreover, as a country with advanced medical and disaster-relief expertise, Israel feels a special responsibility to provide humanitarian assistance to victims around the world. During the 1970s, Israel was one of the few countries in the world willing to take in Vietnamese "boat people" fleeing poverty and war. In addition to rescuing 50,000 Ethiopian Jews from poverty and starvation in the 1980s and 1990s, Israel set up field hospitals, dispatched teams of psychologists, and sent trauma experts to help victims in Rwanda after the brutal tribal war there. In 2004 it provided relief assistance for many devastated by the tsunami in Asia. It recently sent missions to Turkey and Greece after their earthquakes to aid in rescue and medical operations, and sent physicians to help with rescue and relief treatment in flood-devastated Djibouti. Today, Israel is admitting Sudanese refugees who are not allowed to stay in Egypt after fleeing from the genocide in Darfur.

Israel runs the largest program in the world for children who need heart surgery. Named Save a Child's Heart (SACH), Israel has treated more than seven hundred children from Africa, China, and even the Palestinian Authority. Israel helped build hospitals in Gaza, Mauritania, Turkey, and the Ukraine. Finally, Israel conducts almost three hundred courses every year for citizens from developing nations to teach them techniques in desert agriculture, water management, emergency and disaster medicine, refugee absorption, and employment development. Over the years, this program has trained nearly 200,000 participants from more than 130 countries. In providing this humanitarian assistance to people regardless of country, religion, race, or ethnicity, Israel is drawing on the ancient Jewish values of healing the sick and guarding the dignity of every person because all people are created in the image of God.

Israel's achievements in the fields of medicine, science, economics, politics, and high culture as well as its national commitment to help people in need whenever it can are sources of enormous pride to individual Jews. This dedication is eloquent testimony to the talent and energy of the Jewish people when they are allowed to live in their own sovereign country. Because only a government can most effectively harness great technical and organizational expertise and put it to work for the benefit of humanity, only Jewish statehood can fully implement the great biblical and moral values of the Jewish people. Of course, Israel's achievements in these areas and the amount of resources it can dedicate to them are greatly limited by the need to protect itself and its citizens from its enemies. These successes are impressive but only partial in scope. More needs to be done and will be done as Israel continues to grow. Yet the fact that tiny Israel has achieved so much while burdened with nearly sixty years of continuous fighting is nothing less than a modern miracle.

ISRAEL AND JEWS IN THE DIASPORA

The State of Israel makes an essential impact on Jews and Jewish life around the world. The heroic achievements of the young country have filled the hearts of Jews everywhere with a sense of pride. It is no exaggeration to say that Israel has enabled Jews in the Diaspora—and particularly American Jews—to be more confident in identifying publicly as Jews, and given them the courage to effectively defend the Jewish people as a matter of principle. To see the great difference that

Israel has made on their lives, one need only compare the hesitant and unsuccessful pre-State attempts by American Jews to save Europe's Jews from Hitler's Final Solution to the active Jewish public engagement with the American government to defend the lives of Israelis and the security of the Jewish State. In many ways, Israel has allowed American Jews to throw away the insecure policy that the Enlightenment forced on them of "being a Jew at home, but a man in the street." American Jews understand that when they are politically active for Israel and its values of democracy, freedom, and pluralism, they also become better Americans.

Israel has strengthened a vital sense of Jewish identity and peoplehood among Jews everywhere. Jews in America feel bonds of deep connection to Israelis, and this is why for many American Jews, the safety and security of Israel are not merely political interests, but issues related to their very existence. Because Ethiopian, Russian, Yemenite, and Iraqi Jews are living together as equal Israeli citizens, American Jews feel connected to them as brothers and sisters in a way that was never before possible. Because Israel has become a central focus of Jewish identity, thousands of young American Jewish students travel to Israel and look to Israel and its culture to shape their developing consciousness and sense of self. Most American Jews learn Hebrew because it is the native language of one half of all the Jews in the world. Israeli literature and films are popular in Jewish communities around the world, from New York to Buenos Aires to Paris.

Israel has also reconnected many Jews to Jewish tradition and Judaism's ethical values by energizing Diaspora Jews to realize at a higher level the values of charity and giving (*tzedakah*) that are so important to Jewish spiritual life. American Jews have responded with unprecedented generosity to Israel's great needs, donating more than $800 million each year to her various educational, social, cultural, and artistic institutions. By helping to build Israel, American Jews in turn are building themselves into a people with a greater sense of purpose, belonging, and shared values. Israel and its commitment to all Jews everywhere has given American Jewry opportunities to aid Jews abroad wanting to escape poverty, anti-Semitism, and oppression by making *aliyah* (immigration) to Israel. American Jews were intimately involved in helping Jews from Ethiopia, Russia, and Eastern Europe immigrate to the Jewish State. In doing so, American Jews have given life to the ancient rabbinic statement "All Jews are responsible for each other" (Babylonian Talmud, *Shavuot* 39a).

The Jewish State has transformed and revived Jewish identity. Today it is almost inconceivable for American Jews to understand themselves without the presence of Israel, its culture, and its people. As the cultural, religious, and national center of the Jewish people, Israel's influence radiates to Jews everywhere, binding them into a people of shared identity and connectedness.

JEWISH RELIGIOUS ZIONISM AND CHRISTIAN ZIONISM

Ancient Jewish sovereignty on the Land is rooted in God's biblical covenant with the Jewish people. Because modern Israel represents the return of the Jewish people to its biblical homeland, the country has great religious significance to Jews and to many Christians as well. However, it is important to understand that neither the State of Israel, nor its government, nor any Israeli governmental policy or action can be viewed as divinely ordained. From a religious perspective, the modern State of Israel provides only the *opportunity* for the people of

Israel to live out its covenantal values and dreams. Land, sovereignty, and nationhood are necessary historical means, not spiritual ideals in themselves.

Some Jewish religious nationalists and some Christian Zionists see Israel as the confirmation of the biblical redemption and an expression of necessary messianic history. This has led them to the mistake of believing that Israel is invested with divine character that makes it above criticism. Yet modern Israel is made up of human beings of who sometimes err in their struggle to survive, run the country, and live out their destiny. Zionism—even religious Zionism—does not require putting the state and its policies above moral and political criticism. Within Israel itself, political debate and popular criticism are lively and necessary parts of its growing democratic culture. Indeed, no country is above critique, and criticism of Israel and her policies is warranted when it is fair, reasonable, and considers Israel's legitimate need to defend itself and its citizens.

Israel today is very much a country still in development—a human society and imperfect democracy striving to define and live up to its values. Most Israelis and Jews understand the difference between the early religious and secular Zionist thinkers' dreams of building the ideal society that would redeem the Jewish people and the harsh reality of building a state on a land with few natural resources. Because of this difference, Israel's political policies have usually been pragmatic. In addition, since most of Israel's neighbors have rejected the Jewish State as "a foreign implant" in the Middle East that has always been hostile to minorities, non-Muslims, and free societies, Israelis have been forced to focus their primary attention on security and survival. As a result, the project of building the ideal society has become a less urgent immediate value.

In particular, the ongoing war with the Arab world has taught most religious Israelis that merely settling the land of their biblical heritage will not bring redemption or the messianic age, while secular political Zionists have learned that although statehood is necessary for security, peace, and prosperity, it is not sufficient. Everyone familiar with contemporary Israeli life—the brutalizing conflict and the harsh compromises that war demands—understands how far the present reality of Jewish statehood is from the covenantal ideal. From this perspective, the greatest spiritual tragedy of the conflict has been that it has prevented the Jewish people from setting the moral and religious ideals of the covenant as immediate objectives and first priorities.

The issues for the Bible and the Jewish people are not about borders, whether the dust of the Land of Israel is holy, or whether the Land has unique religious properties. Some Jewish mystics and a few religious nationalists have thought this way, but ultimately these ideas were marginalized by Jewish tradition. Today, such extreme thinking is rejected by the overwhelming majority of Israelis and Jews. Only a minuscule percentage of Israelis believe that settlement of the land is more important than democracy, peace, and political compromise with Israel's Arab neighbors. And this tiny percentage of the population does not determine Israeli government policy, as Israel's continuous official commitment to a two-state solution with the Palestinians and unilateral evacuation from Gaza in 2005 indicates. Israelis and rabbinic tradition are more faithful to the biblical ideal of holiness as a product of a just and caring society, rather than something in objects, sites, or lands. They see the ascription of holiness to dust and walls as dangerous idolatries. Sovereignty in the Land returns Judaism and the Jewish people to the political responsibilities of the covenant. If holiness comes from taking responsibility to freely shape a society where covenantal ideals influence behavior and are the primary moral values between people, then political freedom is indispensable to realizing the spiritual vision. This is why the Land and sovereignty are necessary means to the biblical covenant and essential for Jewish self-determination.

8

ISRAEL AND HER ARAB NEIGHBORS

THE CONTINUING CONFLICT

A POPULAR YIDDISH SAYING STATES: "Man plans and God laughs." Both the early religious Zionists, who aspired to rebuild the covenantal ideal in the modern Jewish state, and the secular Zionists, who dreamed of a just Jewish society where Jews would be secure and free from anti-Semitism, never imagined that Israel would be denied the blessings of peace. They knew that there was enough room in Palestine for both Jews and Arabs and believed that a Jewish state could benefit all the inhabitants of the Middle East—Jews and Arabs alike. Yet, tragically, Israel has had to endure nearly sixty years of warfare waged by her Arab neighbors. Even today, Israel is not accepted by most countries in the Middle East, and a new war is an ever-present concern. This ongoing struggle has made an enormous impact on Israeli life and culture, on how Israel is viewed by the rest of the world, and on Israel's ability to realize its goals of justice, equality, and security, both for the Jewish people as a nation and for individual Israelis.

Israel is a tiny country, smaller in geography than the state of New Jersey, and set in the middle of a vast Islamic region. Muslim countries in the Middle East have more than five hundred times as much land as Israel. Israel's population—including

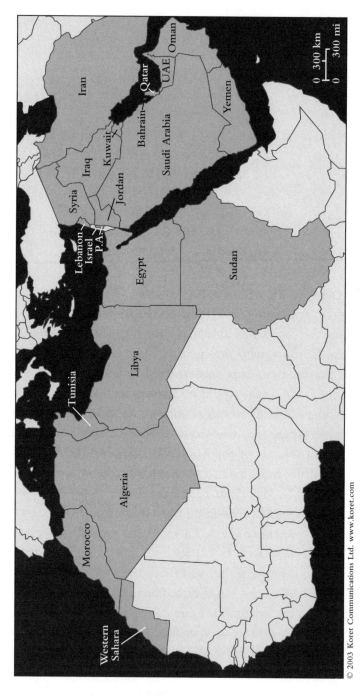

Israel and the Surrounding Region

Israeli Arabs—is only 7,000,000 compared to 300,000,000 Middle Eastern Muslims. Traditional Muslims refer to the Middle East as *Dar al Islam* (the House of Islam) and believe that only Muslim authorities have legitimate control within it.[1] Because of this great imbalance, Israel is strategically and economically vulnerable despite its military strength.

The Arab-Israeli wars have been human, political, and religious tragedies that continue to cause untold suffering to both Jews and Arabs. The disputes have led to different Jewish and Arab narratives, yet certain basic facts are undeniable. They point to three critical differences between Israel and her neighbors that reveal the character of the Jewish State. First, Israel has always had a policy of political pragmatism, accepting compromise and coexistence with Arabs, in contrast to long-standing Arab rejection of Israel's right to exist. Second, Israel fights out of self-defense and is committed to moral standards that minimize war casualties and forbid the intentional harming of innocent parties. In contrast, Arab forces have consistently followed a strategy of attacking Israeli civilians and supporting terrorism. Third, Israel has settled millions of Jewish refugees from abroad—particularly those fleeing persecution in Arab lands—while Arab policy has been to force Palestinian refugees to stay in camps in order to exploit their suffering for political purposes. Israel's policies of political moderation, standards of moral warfare, and responsibility for refugees against great odds come at an enormous human and economic cost. Israel's commitment to these standards indicates the country's progressive values in a region rampant with extremism and violence. They are sources of pride to Jewish people everywhere. Israel's Western values, morality, and political structure explain why it is a vital ally of Western democracies and the free world, even though its Arab enemies control much of the world's oil, so essential to the West.

The fact that Israeli leadership has consistently accepted territorial compromise in Palestine and coexistence with her Arab neighbors, while Arab leaders with a few notable exceptions have rejected coexistence with Israel, is the most important aspect of the ongoing conflict. Of course, there have been Jews who have advocated Jewish control of all of Palestine and Arabs who were willing to concede Israel's right to exist, but these were always minorities and did not determine the active policies of their respective sides. For Arab countries and Palestinians, the dispute has been less about where the borders of Israel should be than whether Israel has had a right to exist at all. This is why peace has been so difficult to achieve and why the conflict has been so hard to resolve through negotiation and compromise. Fundamentally, it is about existence, not territory.

Arab rejection appeared as soon as England's 1917 Balfour Declaration announced that Britain intended to create a Jewish national homeland in Palestine. The local Arab reaction was shock, and violence against Palestinian Jews. Massacres of Jewish civilians took place in Jerusalem, Jaffa, Hadera, Hebron, and other Jewish communities, with hundreds of Jews murdered. In an effort to control Arab violence, the British appointed the grand mufti of Jerusalem, Haj Amin al-Husseini, as the leader of the Palestinian Arabs. Unfortunately, al-Husseini proved to be a public anti-Semite who taught that Jewish rule over any inch of Palestine violated Islamic law and that Islam prohibited Jewish self-determination. He advocated driving most Jews out of Palestine by force and believed only a small number should be allowed to remain as *dhimmis*, or second-class residents under the absolute control of Muslims.[2] Al-Husseini determined Palestinian Arab policy through the 1930s and 1940s, when he became a close ally of Hitler and advocated the Nazi Final Solution. In 1943, he asked Germany to solve the Palestinian Jewish problem the way it was being solved in

Europe and urged Hitler to send the Palestinian Jews to Poland for extermination.[3]

In 1936, Britain established the Peel Commission to study solutions after the Arab rioting broke out against the Jews of Palestine. The commission understood that Jews and Arabs could not live together in one country, and in 1937 recommended partitioning Palestine as the only chance for peace.[4] Under the plan, Jews received only a small proportion of the Palestinian mandate territory, but Jewish leadership nevertheless accepted it. The Arab leaders rejected partition and demanded that most of the Jews be transferred out of the country.[5] Because the Arabs refused "all attempts to give any part of Palestine to Jewish sovereignty,"[6] England retracted the plan and further limited Jewish immigration. Had the partition plan been accepted, millions of Jews would have been able to leave Europe and escape the gas chambers of Auschwitz, Treblinka, and elsewhere.

In 1948, the Arabs again rejected the UN decision of November 1947 to partition Palestine into separate Jewish and Arab states. The Jewish leadership established Israel within the UN-defined borders and requested peace from her neighbors.[7] Although tiny Israel would comprise only one-sixth of 1 percent of the land in the Middle East, the Arab countries absolutely refused to accept the idea of a Jewish State anywhere in the region, and responded by invading Israel and pledging to throw the Jews into the sea. The secretary-general of the Arab League, Azzam Pasha, told the British Broadcasting Company on May 15, 1948, "This will be a war of extermination and a momentous massacre which will be spoken of like the Mongolian massacre and the Crusades." After Israel won the War of Independence, the Arab countries insisted on signing only armistice agreements and still refused to consider the cease-fire lines as legal borders. Once again, Pasha voiced the

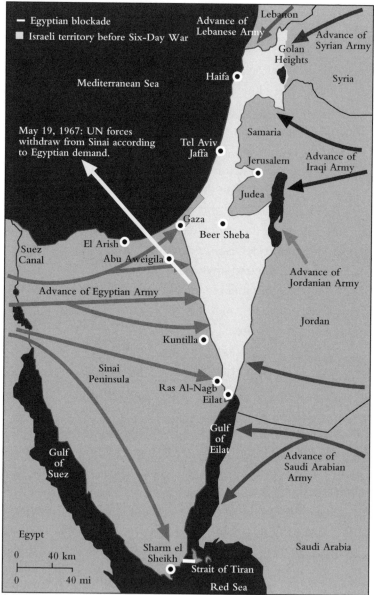

The Events Leading to the Six-Day War, 1967

over-all Arab policy: "We have a secret weapon.... As long as we do not make peace with the Zionists, the war is not over."[8] Jordan occupied the area that the UN plan designated for an Arab state. There was no Arab protest over the Jordanian occupation, since their goal was to block Jewish sovereignty, not to grant Palestinian Arab independence.

Historically, Palestinian Arabs considered themselves part of Greater Syria and never formed any organization promoting Palestinian national identity.[9] The seeds of Palestinian identity were planted in 1964 with the establishment of Palestinian Liberation Organization (PLO). The PLO charter made the organization's goal very clear. It insisted that the United Nations' act of establishing Israel was "null and void" and that the PLO was "to attain the objective of liquidating Israel." The PLO established the Palestinian Liberation Army for the purpose of destroying Israel. It is important to keep in mind that this was three years before Israel conquered the territories of the West Bank and Gaza in the 1967 Six-Day War. The PLO's aim, therefore, was to destroy Israel in its original borders. The PLO determined Palestinian Arab policy until 2006, when the terrorist organization Hamas won the Palestinian elections.

THE SIX-DAY WAR AND PEACE WITH EGYPT AND JORDAN

In May 1967, President Nasser of Egypt once again committed an act of war under international law by closing off the Straits of Tiran to Israeli shipping. Nasser moved 100,000 Egyptian troops through the Sinai desert up to Israel's southern border. At the same time, Syria amassed 75,000 troops on Israel's northern border, and Jordan had another 35,000 troops ready on Israel's border to the east, poised to cut Israel in two at its narrowest point (less than nine miles wide in some places). Jordanian enemy bombers were only minutes away from Tel Aviv, Israel's largest city.

With the Arab countries publicly threatening Israel with invasion and annihilation, Jews around the world feared another Holocaust. Israel turned to America and the European countries to defuse the crisis, but the international community refused to intervene. Israel realized it stood alone and was forced to strike preemptively. In six short days, Israel miraculously destroyed the Egyptian and Syrian air forces, defeated five Arab countries, and captured the Sinai desert from Egypt, the Golan Heights from Syria and the territories on the west bank of the Jordan River. Most important, Israel gained control of the ancient city of Jerusalem, including the Temple Mount and the Western Wall so holy to Jews. Here is what Israeli general Mordechai Gur told his troops after they reclaimed Jerusalem's ancient city:

> For 2,000 years, Jews were barred from the Temple Mount until you, the paratroopers, came and restored it to the bosom of the nation. The Western Wall, for which every Jewish heart yearns, is in our hands again! You have been privileged to complete the circle, to give back to the people their eternal capital and their sacred core.

Israel survived the threat of annihilation, and Jews everywhere celebrated a newfound sense of security. Israel's lightning victory and battlefield bravery dramatically showed the difference between Jewish helplessness twenty-five years earlier when Hitler exterminated six million Jews and the effective Jewish self-defense when Jews had their own country. In a quarter of a century, the Jewish people had risen from the ashes of Auschwitz to become the best air force pilots in the world. Israelis were relieved, but not driven by the quest for power. Israel's chief of staff, Yitzhak Rabin, described the army's attitude after the war:

> Of course we were proud, and we had every right to be—not because we were "invincible" and not because our adversaries were tin soldiers, but because the IDF [Israel Defense Forces] had earned the praise by its professionalism, creativity and sheer obstinacy. We had earned the right to feel confident in our military prowess without denigrating the virtues of our adversaries or falling into the trap of arrogance.[10]

Israel had managed to survive, but Israelis understood that the war was a necessary evil. Peace, not conquest, was still the goal. After capturing Jerusalem's Old City, one Israeli paratrooper reacted to the war this way: "We had to do it. That's all I know. But it must never, never happen again. If it doesn't, then perhaps it will have been worthwhile. But only if it never happens again."[11]

When the war ended, Israel believed that Egypt, Jordan, and Syria would finally be willing to make peace in return for Israeli withdrawal from nearly all the territory Israel conquered. It wanted minor changes to the 1948 cease-fire lines, which its foreign minister, Abba Eban, described as "Auschwitz borders" (see "Israel's Narrow Waistline," p. 138). No country could live with borders that made it nine miles wide and where enemy aircraft could reach its largest cities within five minutes. UN Security Council Resolution 242, passed after the war, recognized this. It required that Israel withdraw from most—but not all—of the territories it had conquered, and only after Arab countries signed a peace treaty and officially renounced war. Israel waited for Egypt, Jordan, and Syria, but the Arab countries again refused to make peace. Their official response came at a meeting of

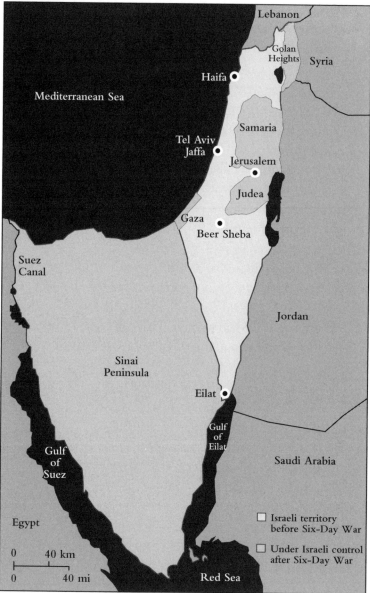

Mediterranean Sea

Lebanon

Golan
Heights

Syria

Haifa

Samaria

Tel Aviv
Jaffa

Jerusalem

Judea

Gaza

Beer Sheba

Suez
Canal

Jordan

Sinai
Peninsula

Eilat

Gulf
of
Eilat

Saudi Arabia

Gulf
of
Suez

Egypt

☐ Israeli territory
before Six-Day War

☐ Under Israeli control
after Six-Day War

0   40 km

0   40 mi

Red Sea

June 10, 1967: Israel After the Six-Day War

the Arab League in Khartoum, Sudan, in 1970: "No peace. No negotiations. No recognition." Once again, the Arab policy of rejection destroyed an opportunity for peace in the region.

Egypt and Syria attacked Israel again in October 1973, on Yom Kippur, the holiest day of the Jewish year. When Egypt's President Anwar Sadat saw that despite suffering heavy losses Israel still succeeded in defeating her enemies, he finally realized that there could be no progress for Egypt until he stopped his hopeless war against Israel. He made a bold decision in 1977 and came to Israel with a promise to negotiate peace. In 1978, Israel and Egypt signed peace agreements at Camp David, with the mediation of the American president, Jimmy Carter. As a result of the peace agreement, Israel withdrew from every inch of occupied Sinai, even though the withdrawal involved evicting Israelis who had made their homes there and giving up vital oil reserves. Jordan made peace with Israel in 1994 and turned Arab responsibility for the West Bank over to the Palestinians.

The Palestinians were also invited to Camp David to make peace with Israel. Israel's prime minister, Menachem Begin, committed himself at the conference to recognizing the legitimate rights of the Palestinians—that is, granting them independence—but the Palestinians still refused to attend or consider peace. This Palestinian refusal represented another missed opportunity for peace, and both Israelis and Palestinians paid a terrible price for this tragic decision by Palestinian leaders. President Sadat's acceptance of Israel was revolutionary in the Arab world. He was later assassinated for breaking ranks with the traditional Arab policy of rejecting Israel, but the peace with both Egypt and Jordan has been stable since the agreements. Unfortunately, Syria, Lebanon, Iraq, Iran, Saudi Arabia, other Muslim countries, and the Palestinians have still refused to make peace with Israel.

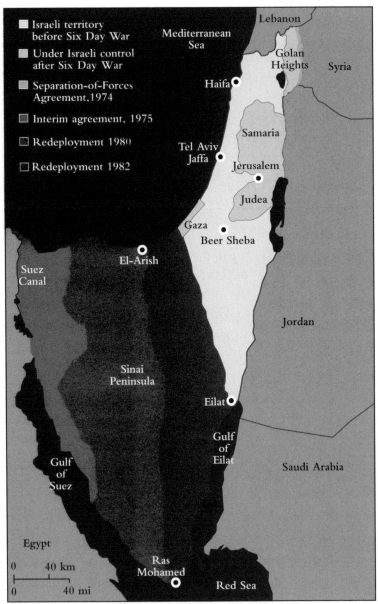

Sinai Redeployment: 1980-1982

SETTLEMENTS AND MESSIANIC HOPES

Many religious Jews in Israel believe in the biblical promise that God gave the entire land of Israel to the Jewish people. Because of this belief, they sought to establish homes in the West Bank, which was conquered by Israel in 1967, and make the territory part of the State of Israel. They interpreted Israel's miraculous victory and Israel's control over the entire biblical homeland as fulfillment of God's promise to Abraham and the advent of the messianic era. This group became known as the "bloc of the faithful" (Gush Emunim) and their vision was that of Greater Israel.

Israel's hopes for peace with the Arab world faded after the Arab League's rejection in Khartoum. Because the Arabs showed no willingness to make peace in return for Israel's withdrawal from territories it conquered, and because these territories are strategically important for Israel's defense, in the 1970s the Israeli government began to support Jewish settlement in the West Bank significantly distant from the Green Line, as the pre-1967 cease-fire lines was called. Yet Israel was careful to never annex this territory and make it a permanent part of Israel. The settler dream of Greater Israel gained momentum and became a movement, but it was never accepted by the majority of Israelis. By the early 1990s, most Israelis, as well as the Israeli government, understood that peace would only be possible when Palestinians were also granted their own state—in other words, when both a Jewish state and a Palestinian state existed between the Mediterranean Sea and the Jordan River. Israel is committed to this two-state solution when it is the result of direct negotiations between Israelis and Palestinians.

The West Bank, which is known to Jews by the biblical names of Judea and Samaria, contains places of great religious and historical significance to the Jewish people. Jerusalem, Hebron, Jericho, Bethlehem, and Nablus are all part of Jewish religious history. The biblical patriarchs and matriarchs of the Jewish people—Abraham and Sarah, Isaac and Rebecca, Jacob and Leah—are buried in Hebron; with the exception of Rachel, who is buried outside Bethlehem. This is the area where Abraham and other Jewish ancestors lived and prayed. Although nearly all Israelis believe that they have historical and religious rights to all of Palestine and that they should be allowed to settle anywhere in this territory, they are willing to sacrifice some of those rights and compromise territorially for the sake of peace with the Palestinians. Since the 1990s, this has been operative Israeli policy, and every government since has committed itself to withdrawing from most of the disputed territories, uprooting Israeli settlements, and accepting a Palestinian state. In the hope of furthering peace and not ruling over the Palestinians, Israel unilaterally evacuated from Gaza in 2005, uprooting 7,000 Israelis who lived there. Unfortunately, the Palestinians responded by electing Hamas, a terrorist organization that ran on a platform of never recognizing Israel and continuing its armed struggle against the Jewish State. Since its election, it has escalated the rocket fire from Gaza into civilian population centers in Israel's south.

Although there are now about 200,000 Israelis living in the disputed territories of the West Bank, approximately 80 percent live in 5 percent of the territory near the Green Line. Under a two-state peace agreement, minor changes to the pre-1967 armistice lines would allow those Israelis to remain in their homes, and the remaining settlers would be relocated into Israel proper. Land exchange from Israel to the new Palestinian state would compensate for the 5 percent of territory retained by Israel. Israelis will agree to the outlines of this two-state solution, however, only when Israel has secure and defensible borders, and when the Palestinians terminate all hostile claims and formally end their warfare and terrorism against Israel by signing a peace treaty.

OSLO AND THE FAILED PEACE PROCESS

Throughout the 1990s, Israel—and the world—held out hope that the Palestinian Authority, led by Yasir Arafat, would finally agree to a compromise solution, end its campaign of terror against Israeli civilians, and sign a peace agreement with Israel. The Oslo Accords outlined a two-state solution and a process leading to Palestinian statehood. Israel followed the accords and began withdrawing from Arab cities and occupied territories. Finally, the reality of a lasting peace to prosper both Israelis and Palestinians seemed near. The moment of truth came in 2000 at negotiations, first at Camp David and then at Taba, Egypt, when then president Bill Clinton offered his peace proposals to Israeli and Palestinian leaders. Israel's prime minister, Ehud Barak accepted the offer, agreeing that Israel would withdraw from all of Gaza and 95 percent of the West Bank, give the Palestinians an additional 2 percent of land from Israel, accept a Palestinian state in contiguous West Bank territory,[12] recognize a district of East Jerusalem as the capital of the new Palestinian state, dismantle Israeli settlements, and relocate Israeli settlers.[13] It was a generous offer made at great sacrifice to Israeli religious, strategic, and political interests. Yet Barak and Israelis considered it worth the goal of peace.

However, Arafat could not bring himself to accept the offer or sign a peace agreement with Israel and renounce terror. He rejected Clinton's proposals and made no counteroffer.[14] Instead, he launched the intifada, a violent armed terror campaign in Jerusalem, Tel Aviv, Haifa, and Netanya that has savagely murdered more than 1,000 Israelis—most of them

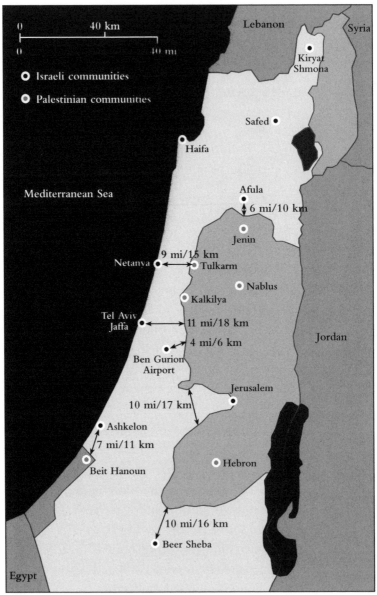

Israel's Narrow Waistline

civilians.[15] As President Clinton said after the negotiations failed, Israel was prepared to take bold risks and compromise, and the Palestinians were not. Once again, Israeli pragmatism and moderation were met with Arab rejection and intolerance of the Jewish State in the Middle East. Another opportunity for peace and prosperity was lost. Thousands of Israelis and Palestinians continue to die because of Arafat's rejection of peace at Taba.

Since the breakdown of the Oslo Accords, dark trends have appeared in the Middle East. The terrorist group Hamas now controls the Palestinian government. It is committed to building an Islamic state in all of Palestine. It is fueling violence from Gaza against Israelis in southern Israeli cities and smuggling in arms from Egypt and other Arab countries. Another Islamic party practicing terrorism, Hezbollah, has gained political strength in Lebanon to Israel's north and is armed with military equipment from Syria and Iran for use against Israel. Islamic fundamentalists now rule Iran and are working to acquire nuclear weapons. The president of Iran, Mahmoud Ahmadinejad, has questioned whether the Holocaust really happened and publicly stated that Israel should be wiped off the map. All these Islamist groups accept only Muslim authority in *Dar al Islam*. They refuse to accept the right of Israel to exist and have publicly vowed to destroy the Jewish state when it is possible to do so. Islamist fundamentalism is rising today in the Palestinian territories, Lebanon, Iran, Iraq, and Syria, dealing a severe setback to prospects for peace in the Middle East and opposing Israel's Western spirit of moderation and pragmatism. The rise in Islamic extremism and Arab terror has increased Israel's vulnerability and its legitimate need for self-defense.

To protect its citizens, Israel has been forced to build a security fence separating Israelis from Palestinians in the hope

Map Reflecting Clinton Ideas

Proposed Palestinian State

Israeli Settlement Blocs Annexed to Israel

MEDITERRANEAN SEA

0   15
miles

N

Haifa

Sea of Galilee

Jordan River

Jenin

Tulkarm

Nablus

Qalqilya

Tel Aviv

WEST BANK

Ramallah

Jericho

Jerusalem   Maale Adumim

ISRAEL

Bethlehem

Gaza

Hebron

GAZA STRIP

Dead Sea

JORDAN

EGYPT

No formal map was presented to the Israelis and Palestinians in December 2000 by President Clinton, but this map illustrates the Clinton ideas—a Palestinian state in 95% of the West Bank and 100% of Gaza. This map actually understates the Clinton ideas by not showing an additional 1 to 3% of territorial swaps to the Palestinian state from areas within Israel.

Map of the Palestinian State according to
Clinton's Ideas at Taba Negotiations

of preventing Palestinian terrorists from entering Jewish population centers and murdering Israeli civilians. Ninety-five percent of the barrier is a fence and 5 percent is a wall; it has succeeded in reducing terrorist deaths by more than 85 percent. The barrier has severely disrupted Palestinian life, and even Israelis prefer that it not extist. Yet it is a necessary step that is preferable to suicide bombers blowing up buses in Tel Aviv, killing Israeli children eating pizza in Jerusalem restaurants, and murdering Israelis participating in a Passover seder in Netanya. Palestinian terror created the need to build the fence, and only when Palestinian terror stops will the fence come down. Although it is not a political border, the fence is stark testimony to the tragedy, suffering, and destruction that the Arab war on Israel has caused for both Israelis and Palestinians.

FIGHTING A MORAL WAR

The second critical difference between Israel and her enemies is the way each side fights in wartime. Israel has always seen the battle as one between armies and armed soldiers, and it refuses to specifically target civilians. Israel's Arab enemies, however, have a policy of intentionally murdering innocent Israeli women and children because their aim is to disrupt and destroy Israeli society. In other words, Israel has tried to fight according to moral standards and Western principles of just war, while Arab countries and the Palestinians have regularly adopted a policy of terrorism against Israelis.

Of course, war is tragic, and both innocent Israelis and Arabs have died in the conflict. Yet there is a vast moral difference between the unintentional deaths of innocent bystanders caused by Israeli military operations and the intentional murder of Israeli women and children for political purposes by militant

Arabs. Israel's objective is self-defense, and unintended civilan deaths are an unfortunate but necessary evil in the fight to protect life. Israel works actively to minimize civilian casualties, while terrorists intentionally murder innocent people and deny the sacred value of human life. In 2007, a Hamas leader told the *Washington Post*, "Palestinians have Israelis on the run now because they have found their weak spot: Jews love life more than other people, and they prefer not to die. Suicide bombers are ideal for dealing with them." It is no accident that suicide bombings, blowing up airplanes, bombing of buses and trains—in fact, the general scourge of terrorism now threatening Western societies—have all been used first against Israel.[16] It is clear that Israel and the West stand together against common terrorist enemies.

The number of Israelis murdered by Arab terrorists far exceeds the number of unarmed Arab bystanders killed unintentionally by Israel. Now that Egypt and Jordan have made peace with Israel, the main terrorist threat comes from Palestinian forces, and the secondary threat comes from Hezbollah in Lebanon. During the second intifada, from 2001 to 2003, the *Boston Globe* reported that 18 percent of Palestinians killed were noncombatants.[17] During that period, 80 percent of the eight hundred Israelis killed were innocent civilians, most of them women, children, and elderly people. Israeli female fatalities outnumbered Palestinian ones by four to one.[18] This is because the Palestinians purposely went after women and children and sought to maximize death by putting nails in their bombs and sometimes even soaking them in rat poison.[19] This massive assault on innocent Israelis has strengthened their belief that the Palestinian leadership seeks Israel's annihilation.

Despite the terrorist tactics of Palestinians, Israel's army fights under a code called "The Purity of Arms," which obligates

Israeli soldiers to minimize needless deaths and forbids them from targeting civilians. It demands that "a soldier shall use his weapons and force to the degree needed to subdue the enemy, but will exercise restraint to avoid unnecessary injury to a person's life, his person, honor, or property."[20] Israel's citizens and military make mistakes and sometimes violate this code. When Israeli groups or individuals commit acts that intentionally harming Arab civilians, however, such actions are examined, condemned, and prosecuted by the Israeli army and authorities.[21] They are violations of Israeli law and values that deeply embarrass Israelis. As a result of this policy, Israel has killed fewer innocents in proportion to its own civilians killed than any country in a comparable war. Moreover, Israel is the only country whose judiciary actively enforces the rule of law against its army during wartime.[22]

MIDDLE EAST REFUGEES

The third critical difference between Israel and her Arab neighbors has been in the treatment of war refugees. In any war, people living in the battle areas flee. World War II produced tens of millions of refugees, and the 1948 war between India and Pakistan caused twleve million people to move from one country to another. That same year, between 475,000 and 750,000 Arabs fled Israel during the War of Independence—a war Israel didn't want and didn't begin. A minority of Arabs left because they were expelled from strategic areas by the Israeli army. Generally, however, Israel urged its Arabs to remain in order to help block the invasion by Arab countries. Here is the Federation of Jewish Workers' appeal to Haifa's Arabs: "Do not leave. Do not bring tragedy upon yourselves by unnecessary evacuation. By moving out, you will be overtaken by poverty and humiliation."[23] One hundred and sixty thousand Arabs chose peace and stayed in the Jewish state;[24] many more fled because Arab leaders broadcasted instructions to leave to make invasion and the slaughter of the Israelis easier. The Syrian prime minister at the time, Haled al Azm, admitted: "We ourselves are the ones who encouraged them to leave. Only a few months separated our call to them to leave and our appeal to the UN to resolve their return."[25] Many other Arabs left simply to flee the violence of the war begun by the invading Arab countries.

The millions of refugees from World War II as well as those from India and Pakistan have all been resettled and are citizens of their new countries. But the Arab world has insisted on permanent refugee status for the Palestinians and refused them citizenship in their own Arab countries. From 1948 to 1967, when Egypt and Jordan controlled the Gaza Strip and the West Bank, both those countries kept the Palestinians in refugee camps even as the refugee population swelled, becoming increasingly poorer and more desperate. In 1958, Ralph Galloway, the former director of the United Nations Relief Works Agency (the UN agency responsible for the refugees), explained, "The Arab states do not want to solve the refugee problem. They want to keep it an open sore, as an affront to the UN and as a weapon against Israel."[26] Jordan's King Hussein later admitted the motive for mistreating the refugees: "Since 1948 Arab leaders have used the Palestinian people for selfish purposes."[27] As long as the refugees were unsettled, Arabs could blame Israel for injustice, continuing the political war against Israel by preserving Palestinian suffering and poverty to use as rationales for the need to reclaim Israeli land.

The United Nations assumed responsibility for the refugees, and in 2005 estimated that there were 4,300,000 of them. Even when the PLO controlled the Gaza Strip, it never dismantled the refugee camps. At the 2001 Taba negotiations, Israel offered to help raise $30 billion to settle the refugees in the proposed Palestinian state, yet the Palestinian leaders refused. The Arabs still demand that these refugees have the right to return to their original homes in Israel, which of course would flood the country with Arabs and undermine Israel's Jewish character. In other words, the refugee problem has been left deliberately unresolved by the Arabs as a continuing tactic to destroy Israel.

This cynical and cruel policy is in marked contrast to how Israel settled approximately the same number of Jews, who fled persecution in Muslim countries in the years after Israel was created. Israel struggled to absorb close to 300,000 European Jews and 600,000 Jews from Middle East countries, give them citizenship, and integrate them into the new society. Israel is proud that it could provide these Jews with a new life and considers absorbing Jewish refugees a national moral obligation. Today, hundreds of thousands of Jews from Algeria, Egypt, Iran, Iraq, Morocco, Tunisia Syria, Yemen, and Libya are productive and secure citizens of Israel.

Israel has made both political and humanitarian mistakes in trying to fight a moral war against her Arab enemies. Certainly the Palestinian people are suffering terribly—much of which has been caused by Palestinian leaders' own rejection of compromise solutions for peace. Israel feels a moral obligation to minimize Palestinian suffering, yet Israel is fully justified in building its military strength and using it defensively against enemies who are bent on her destruction. The Holocaust taught the Jewish people that powerlessness is evil because it leads to extermination and genocide. Although it is not easy to manage, having power and using it morally is the Jewish and Israeli ideal. As a people of the covenant and its moral values, Israel can be held to high ethical standards, but not to the impossible and even suicidal ones that some demand only for the Jewish State and for no other country in the world.

Israelis understand that like all people, Palestinians have a right to peace and prosperity. The only way for both Jews and Palestinians to live and prosper is for each to have its own state that coexists in peace, recognizes the other, and no longer makes belligerent claims. Israel yearns to achieve this two-state solution through rational negotiation, mutual acceptance, and fair compromise. A solid majority of Israelis agree to this vision of compromise and moderation, and Israeli governments have adopted it as their fundamental approach to the Palestinians.

When Arabs agree in principle to recognition and coexistence with Israel, both peoples will share the blessings of peace and prosperity. The first signs that Arabs truly accept these principles will be when they cease their policy of terror and incitement against Israelis, stop demanding that Palestinians return to Israel, dismantle the refugee camps, and settle Arab refugees outside of the Jewish State. When Israel's Arab neighbors take these steps, they will find Israel an enthusiastic proponent of turning conflict into cooperation, an eager partner for peace, and a tireless worker in bringing prosperity to all the residents of the Middle East.

PART IV

THE FUTURE AND THE HOPE

9

ISRAEL OF TOMORROW: THE MEANING OF ISRAEL FOR WORLD VALUES AND CULTURE

THE CONTINUING SPIRITUAL CHALLENGE

As we have seen, the existence of the Jewish State has transformed the Jewish people from a scattered and vulnerable people to a strong and free nation. Jews are now able to protect themselves and have assumed responsibility for their character as a people. Israel has taken Jewish sacred history, peoplehood, and ethics out of the realm of speculation and put them into the crucible of real life experience. In returning the Jewish people to its homeland, Israel has also returned Jews to material reality—with all its challenges. In brief, the Jewish people's return to the Land returns Judaism to its original vision and the Jewish people to the responsibilities of the biblical covenant.

As Israel continues to develop as a nation, to defend herself and provide a home to Jews everywhere, and as she attempts to find acceptance by her neighbors in the Middle East, the larger spiritual challenge is to be faithful to the moral and spiritual ideals of the biblical covenant to be a blessing to humanity ("all the nations of the earth" [Genesis 12:3 and 18:8]) and a model for justice and righteousness to the world. Somehow,

Israel must resist becoming just another Levantine state like the other countries of the Middle East, and find a way to be a light unto the nations, influencing the culture, morality, and religions around the world.

The ongoing drama of Israeli life is dominated by its struggle for survival and security and its spiritual challenge for the Jewish people to realize its religious mission on the Land to become a kingdom of priests and a holy people that models its covenantal values for all humanity. These two continuing efforts—the political and the spiritual—are related.

What will the society look like when the covenantal destiny is achieved? What is the vision of the "end of days," when holiness suffuses the world and the Jewish mission is fulfilled? Micah (4:1–5) describes covenantal fulfillment with stunning beauty:

> In the end of days to come;
> the Mount of the Lord's house shall stand
> Firm above the mountains;
> And it shall be a tower above the hills.
> The peoples shall gaze onto it with joy;
> And the many nations shall go and say:
> "Come,
> Let us go up to the Mount of the Lord,
> To the House of the God of Jacob;
> That He may instruct us in His ways,
> And that we may walk in His paths.
> For instruction shall come forth from Zion,
> The word of the Lord from Jerusalem....
> And they shall beat their swords into plowshares
> And their spears into pruning hooks.
> Nation shall not take up
> Sword against nation;

They shall never again know war;
But every man shall sit under his grapevine or fig tree
With no one to disturb him.
For it was the Lord of Hosts who spoke.
Though all the peoples walk.
Each in the name of its gods,
We will walk
In the name of the Lord our God
Forever and ever.

This is the messianic dream of universal recognition of God's authority, of obedience to moral values, of peace for all, and of personal and national security. Peace and security are natural concomitants of spiritual success, for respect for God's authority entails relating with reverence to all people who are created in God's holy image. Micah concludes with a startling claim of theological pluralism: "Though all the peoples walk, Each in the name of its gods." There is no mass conversion to one universal religion or church, only recognition and tolerance of each people's right to understand God on its own terms. The world is neither exclusively Jewish, nor Christian, nor Muslim. Jerusalem is a place of social and religious diversity, not a monolithic Jewish society where everyone calls God by the same name. Jerusalem is a place where Jews and gentiles coexist in harmony, respecting each other and worshiping alongside each other in faithfulness to their respective spiritual traditions.

Jerusalem, Israel, and, by extension, all the earth is to be a place where Jews, Christians, Muslims, indeed all people, live in faith and blessing. Religion is not a zero-sum game in which one group attains dignity at the cost of the others. Jews are charged by God to somehow bring about this ideal state of affairs, to be the agents "through whom all of the families of the earth shall be blessed" (Genesis 12:3 and 18:8). And

Christians who see themselves as heirs to the Abrahamic covenant also participate in this divine responsibility.

Consider the significance of the State of Israel, particularly in the heart of the Middle East. What role has Israel played thus far in religious and cultural history? All agree that the Holocaust was the prime catalyst for the recent change in Christian theology regarding Jews and Judaism. Yet few historical changes are monocausal, and the undeniable reality of the State of Israel has also influenced Christian thinking about Jews. In providing the Jewish people with strength and political reality, Israel has allowed the Jewish people to be taken seriously among the family of nations. In giving the Jewish people a corporate dimension, Israel has also helped to equalize relations between Christians and Jews, leveling the playing field between Jews and the churches, whether the Vatican, the Orthodox church, or the various Protestant churches.

Second, the old Augustinian doctrine of the Jews serving as negative witness to Christianity insisted that God decreed Jews to remain homeless and abased, as punishment for their rejection of Jesus. But this humiliating teaching of contempt could not be maintained after 1948, when Jews returned to their biblical homeland. The permanence of the State of Israel is a powerful empirical refutation of this thesis that has caused so much Christian persecution and Jewish suffering throughout the ages. Ultimately, after much soul-searching, Christian churches acknowledged the Jewish State's right to exist and thereby implicitly rejected the old doctrine. Christian recognition of Israel—even when officially restricted to a political level—cannot totally avoid religious implications. Such recognition necessarily strengthens the idea that the Jewish covenant can no longer be seen as an "old" covenant, but rather must be viewed as a living one. It implies that for Jews Judaism remains a valid path to God.

Some Christians have difficulty understanding the eternal Jewish attachment to the Land of Israel. Unlike in the Old Testament, land does not play a prominent role in Christian Scripture, and there is no similar concept of peoplehood in Christian religious thought. As mentioned in chapter 1, this led early Christian religious thinkers to see the biblical category of the Land as a metaphor and to substitute the body of Christ for it. Yet, because the Land of Israel was the home of the biblical patriarchs and matriarchs as well as the place where Jesus lived and died, the Jewish homeland always remained very special to Christians and continues to be so today. Another factor is the Protestant Reformation's protest against the abusive temporal power of the Catholic Church, which led to a Protestant tenet that religion should be completely divorced from state power. This partially explains why some Protestant theologians and churches feel uncomfortable today with the idea of Jewish statehood and Israeli power. But while doctrinally understandable, the effort to denationalize Judaism misunderstands Judaism and the experience of the Jewish people, and it unfairly forces Judaism into a Protestant mold. This misconception can lead to harsh critiques of Zionism and Israel's policies toward the Palestinians. Some of the criticism is fair and responsible, some is oblivious to legitimate Israeli security concerns, while some—as it relates to Palestinian liberation theology, for example—is anti-Zionist and even anti-Semitic.[1]

JEWS AND CHRISTIANS AS PARTNERS IN THE FUTURE

A true understanding of Israel and its religious significance should bring Christians and Jews closer together. Now that Christians have rejected supersessionism and understand that Judaism and Christianity have a common spiritual patrimony, many Christian thinkers—liberal and evangelical, Protestant and Catholic—see the return of the Jewish people to their biblical homeland as strengthening Christian sacred history and the Jewish covenant on which Christian faith rests. The largest Protestant church in Germany recognized this, proclaiming: "The return to the Land of Promise, and also the creation of the State of Israel, are signs of the faithfulness of God toward his people."[2] So did the Dutch Reformed Church: "It is a sign for us that it is God's will to be on earth together with man. Therefore we rejoice in this reunion of [the Jewish] people and land."[3]

The return of the Jewish people to their covenantal homeland is a significant theological event that strengthens the foundations of Christian faith and mission. Many individual Protestant and Catholic thinkers, among them James Parkes, Petra Heldt, Marcel Dubois, and John Pawlikowski, understand that the Land and its history are critically important to modern Christian identity.[4] Another prominent Christian thinker, Helmut Gollwitzer, put it well:

> Israel's homecoming creates so many new possibilities in the relationship between the Church and Israel that we can hardly be alert enough and grateful enough. We shall therefore have to realize that whatever hits Israel must also pierce the very heart of the Church.[5]

This link needs to be developed further by Christian thinkers. Israel, then, holds the potential for Christians to better understand and affirm their faith with its roots in the Jewish covenant.

To the Muslim world, Israel as a sovereign Jewish state represents the possibility of non-Muslim legitimacy and even equality in *Dar Al Islam*. This is new and threatening to traditional Islamic culture. Scholars of Middle East history agree that there has never been a concept of equality for non-Muslims in traditional Arab society.[6] Jews and Christians have always been considered *dhimmis*, second-class residents who are sometimes protected and sometimes abased but never equal to Muslims in law or social status. This explains why there is such fierce rejection of Israel by Arabs throughout the Middle East. The conflict is not primarily a territorial dispute between Israelis and Palestinians. Why should an imam in Mecca care who is responsible for the garbage collection of Tel Aviv? To Muslims in Mecca, Teheran, and Cairo, Israel represents the end to monolithic Muslim control of the Middle East, the end to the traditional Islamic conception of exclusivist politics and religious superiority in that part of the world.

After the Holocaust, Jews demanded they not be second-class residents whose fate depended on the benevolence of others. They understood that the only place Jews could be secure and have any chance to realize their age-old dreams was in their own Jewish state. As such, Israel represents the principle of pluralism in the Middle East. It is the ongoing test of whether non-Muslims can be equal in that part of the world, whether they need not be subordinate to Muslim sufferance, whether they can take responsibility for their own well-being, and whether they can be free to shape their distinctive identity.

Because traditional Middle East societies regard minorities with suspicion and deny them equality, Jews and Christians as threatened minorities share a common challenge in the region. Can they live with equality and dignity alongside the overwhelming majority of Muslims? The central ideological and religious question of the tragic conflict is precisely this: Will the Middle East be an intolerant world in which only Muslims have legitimacy and respectful place, or will it be the venue for Micah's dream, where many peoples live in dignity, security, and peace?

In this time of rising Islamic nationalism throughout the Middle East, Christians in Lebanon, Egypt, Iran, Iraq, and the Palestinian territories are suffering from religious intolerance. Four of every five Maronite Christians have left Lebanon. Nearly all Christians have left Iraq, and in Egypt twelve million Copts experience discrimination and harassment daily. Bibles are forbidden in Saudi Arabia, and even American soldiers are not permitted to wear a cross in public or display any signs of their Christian faith. Conversion to Christianity is a capital crime in many Muslim countries. Most Christians who have enough money are leaving the region, primarily because of this Islamic intolerance.[7] Democratic and pluralistic Israel remains the one safe haven for Christians and their holy sites in the Middle East.

As Israel takes root in the Middle East, the principle of non-Muslim legitimacy and equality will become more accepted in the region. When this occurs, Christians, too, will necessarily be seen as belonging to the region, and their rights, interests, and welfare will become more secure. Today both Jews and Christians are Middle East minorities who are considered *dhimmis*, and this common status makes them strategic allies with common challenges and a common message. The battle is not between Islam on one side and Judaism and Christianity on the other. Neither is it between Muslims and Jews, or between Muslims and Christians. The real physical and spiritual battle is between extremists of all faiths who hate diversity and difference, and moderates with Micah's pluralistic dream. Israel is the front line of the cultural and moral war that will determine whether the Middle East will be a place of monistic intolerance or pluralistic blessing. This is why the conflict is so great, and why it transcends the Israeli and Palestinian communities to vitally affect all Jews, Christians, Sunni, and Shiite and Sufi Muslims, Baha'is, and all minorities—indeed, all who cherish the covenant, freedom, and human dignity.

As an evolving democracy with a modern economy in a region of harsh dictatorial rule, Israel is a powerful witness to the values of modernity, freedom, and human rights for all people in the Middle East. It can help bring democracy, liberty, and equality to the region, not by military conquest or violent change, but by providing an example of how human life prospers and how different human beings can live together with dignity in a society that celebrates these values. As a model of freedom, knowledge, and tolerance, Israel can fulfill Isaiah's charge spoken in God's name, "You are My witnesses" (Isaiah 43:11–12).

Christians and Jews who believe in the messianic hope are obligated to believe in Micah's dream and to work to make it a reality. We are not allowed to despair and fall prey to a hopelessness born of confining our vision to the brutal politics of the day. Like the biblical Queen Esther in ancient Persia, perhaps God has put Jews and Christians in this tragic situation of constant violence, which breaks so many hearts and destroys so many of God's images, precisely so we can work for Micah's vision. Somehow we must create the possibility for Jews, Christians, and Muslims, for Buddhists and Hindus, all to call the God of the universe in their own names, and for the peoples of the region to beat their swords into plowshares, transforming their instruments of destruction into vessels of creativity and blessing. That is the challenge of the covenant and, with God's help, one of the great roles that the State of Israel can play in human history.

NOTES

INTRODUCTION

1. Throughout this book, the general term "Bible" refers to Hebrew Scriptures. References to Christian Scriptures, sometimes called the New Testament, will be explicitly noted.

CHAPTER 1

1. Since the birth of Jesus is not a significant point in Jewish history, Jews divide history between the Common Era (CE) and Before the Common Era (BCE), which correspond to AD and BC, respectively.
2. Through the prophet Isaiah, God calls Israel "My witnesses" (Isaiah 43:11–12). The Rabbis derived the *midrash* from the text of Genesis 24:2–3. See *Sifre, Ha'azinu* 313 and David Hartman, *A Living Covenant: The Innovative Spirit in Traditional Judaism* (Woodstock, VT: Jewish Lights Publishing, 1998), pp. 28–30.
3. It is unfortunate that *Torah* is traditionally translated as "law" in Christian documents. This is derived from the Septuagint translation of the Hebrew Torah into Greek, where Torah was translated as *nomos*. Jewish tradition never understood *Torah* as exclusively legal. The more literal translation, "teaching," is more accurate, since Jewish Scriptures contain—and always have been understood by Jews to be—a combination of law, ethics, and narrative.

4. See Isaiah 5:14–17, and Eliezer Berkovits, *Essential Essays on Judaism*, David Hazony, ed. (Jerusalem: Shalem Press, 2002), pp. 255–56.

CHAPTER 2

1. See the critical document of the Second Vatican Council, *Nostra Aetate*, Section 4, found at http://www.vatican.va/archive/hist_councils/ii_vatican_council/documents/vat-ii_decl_19651028_nostra-aetate_en.html. All major Protestant churches have also acknowledged these principles.

2. For a full description of this development, see Robert Wilkin, *The Land Called Holy* (New Haven: Yale University Press, 1992), ch. 4.

3. Both the Hebrew prophets (Jeremiah 32:40 and Hosea 2:21–22) state this as well as Paul in Christian Scriptures. See Paul's Letter to the Romans, chapter 11.

4. Deuteronomy 5 and 30 capture this historical dynamic best:

Stand here by Me and I will speak to you about all the commandments, the statutes and the judgments that you shall teach them, so that they may observe them *in the Land that I gave them to possess.*... You shall walk in all the ways that the Lord has commanded you, so that you may live and be well and *lengthen your days on the Land that you possess* [emphasis mine]. (5:28)

When all these things befall you—the blessing and the curse that I have set before you—you shall take them to heart among the nations into which the Lord your God has driven you. You shall return to the Lord your God and shall obey his voice according to all that I command you this day—you and your children, with all your heart and with all your soul. Then the Lord our God ... will gather you from

all the nations among whom the Lord your God has scattered you.... *And the Lord your God will bring you to the Land
that your fathers possessed, and you shall possess it.* (30:1–5)

5. Famous Christians and Jews alike have written about this difference. See Matthew Arnold's celebrated essay, "Hebraism and
Hellenism," in *Culture and Anarchy* (London: Smith, Elder, 1869);
and Leo Strauss, "Jerusalem and Athens," in *Jewish Philosophy and
the Crisis of Modernity* (Albany: SUNY Press, 1997).

6. In Judaism, sexuality becomes holy first by helping to relieve the
existential loneliness that hinders connectedness to both other
people and the Divine; since a committed love relationship
between man and woman is seen as the most concrete symbol
of the union between a person and God. Secondarily, it is sanctified as the means of propagation by which God's covenantal
partners continue their responsibilities throughout history.
Celibacy is a sin in Jewish law.

7. Food plays a central role in Jewish religious life. There is vir-
tually no Jewish religious celebration for which Jewish tradition does not mandate a public festive meal. As a primary
human experience, eating cannot escape the religious need for
sanctification. Judaism attempts this through the demands of
kashrut, which are designed to condition control over primitive biological impulses. Blessings over food and the entire system of kashrut are attempts to set a place for God at the dinner
table.

8. The Sabbath and holidays are also sanctified in physical ways:
with intimacy, food, wine, music, and social relations.

9. Death is associated with ritual impurity—the antithesis of holiness—because death represents the termination of the potential
to infuse the body with spirit. While still retaining traces of the
image of God, in the end a corpse is only a physical entity no
longer capable of experiencing the Divine. Hence Judaism
always understood death as a tragic event ending the covenantal
responsibility of that person to bring God onto the earth.

CHAPTER 3

1. Many Jews and some Rabbis thought Bar Kochba was the messiah who could bring redemption and independence to the Jewish people. When he was killed without achieving this, his followers understood that he could not be the messiah.
2. Yehezkel Kaufman, in *Great Ages and Ideas of the Jewish People,* Leo W. Schwarz, ed. (New York: Random House, 1956), p. 31.
3. Ibid., p. 32.
4. This idea was popularized by Judah Halevi in his famous medieval work, *The Kuzari* (New York: Schocken, 1964), part I.
5. See the essays by Matthew Arnold and Leo Strauss, Chapter 2, note 5.
6. Ralph Marcus, "The Hellenistic Age," in *Great Ideas of the Jewish People,* Leo W. Schwarz, ed. (New York: Random House, 1956), pp. 138–39.
7. See Babylonian Talmud, *Shabbat* 31a.
8. James Parkes, *End of An Exile: Israel, the Jews and the Gentile World,* Roberta Kalechofsky and Eugene Korn, eds. (Marblehead, MA: Micah Publications, 2005), p. 26.

CHAPTER 4

1. The Talmud is a vast corpus of rabbinic discussion containing law, ethics, narrative and parable. After the destruction of the Temple, the Talmud became the most important source of Jewish law and development of Jewish life in the Diaspora. It laid the foundation for rabbinic Judaism and even today, it constitutes the fundamental source of legal discussion, ethical guidance, and normative standards among Orthodox Jews.
2. See Joseph Bernardin, "Anti-Semitism: A Catholic Critique" in *Toward Greater Understanding,* Anthony J. Cernera, ed. (Fairfield, CT: Sacred Heart University, 1995), pp. 18–19.
3. Ibid., p. 19.

4. Jules Isaac, *The Teaching of Contempt: Christian Roots of Anti-Semitism* (New York: McGraw-Hill, 1965).

5. Edward Flannery, *The Anguish of the Jews: Twenty-three Centuries of Anti-Semitism* (Mahwah, NJ: Paulist Press, 1999); and Malcolm Hay, *Thy Brother's Blood: The Roots of Christian Anti-Semitism* (New York: Hart Publishing, 1975).

6. Israel Abrahams, *Jewish Life in the Middle Ages* (New York: Atheneum, 1969), p. 62.

7. Jacob R. Marcus, *The Jew in the Medieval World* (New York: Atheneum, 1969), p. 137

8. Ibid., p. 139.

9. Ibid., p. 43.

10. H. H. Ben Sasson, *The History of the Jewish People* (Cambridge, MA: Harvard University Press, 1976), p. 650.

11. Ibid., p. 413.

12. Ibid., p. 465.

13. Ibid.

14. Marcus, pp. 51–55.

15. Ibid., p. 75–78.

Chapter 5

1. Howard M. Sachar, *The Course of Modern Jewish History* (New York: Random House, 1990), pp. 27–29.

2. Ibid., p. 29.

3. Ibid., p. 51.

4. Quoted in Ben Sasson, p. 745.

5. Count Stanislaus de Clermon-Tonnerre (a member of the French National Assembly), December 23, 1789. See Raphael Mahler, *A History of Modern Jewry 1780–1815* (New York: Schocken, 1971), p. 32.

6. Sachar, p. 73.

7. Ibid., p. 78.

8. Ben Sasson, p. 814.

9. As quoted in Sachar, p. 215.

10. Ibid., p. 222.

11. Ben Sasson, p. 861.

12. Ibid., p. 655.

13. Dore Gold, "Jerusalem in International Diplomacy: Demography," *Jerusalem Center for Public Affairs*, October 27, 2006.

14. Arieh Avneri, *The Claim of Dispossession*, 4th ed. (Transaction, 2005).

15. Leon Pinsker, *Auto-Emancipation: An Appeal to His People by a Russian Jew*, trans. D. S. Blondheim (New York: Masada, 1939), p. 12.

16. Interim Report on the Civil Administration of Palestine to the League of Nations, June 1921.

17. Rashid Khalidi, *Palestinian Identity* (New York: Columbia University Press, 1998), pp. 112–13.

18. See Jacob De Haas, *Palestine: The Last Two Thousand Years* (New York: Macmillan, 1934), pp. 368 and 407.

19. According to the French study by Vital Cuinet, Syrian, Libyan and Palestinian Geographical Administrative Statistics (Paris 1896), pp. 583–84.

20. The area from the Jordan River to the Mediterranean Sea, or what was to become Palestine after the creation of Transjordan in 1922.

21. Walter Laqueur, *A History of Zionism* (New York: Schocken Books, 1989), p. 510.

22. Quoted in Sachar, *The Course of Modern Jewish History* (New York: Random House, 1990), p. 270.

23. Letter from Lord Arthur J. Balfour, British foreign secretary, to Lord Rothschild, president of the British Zionist Federation. Quoted in Sachar, *History of Israel*, p. 109.

24. Some excellent histories are Raul Hilberg, *The Destruction of European Jewry* (New Haven: Yale University Press, 2003); Lucy Davidowicz, *The War Against the Jews: 1933–1945* (New York: Holt, Rinehart and Winston, 1975); and Martin Gilbert, *The Holocaust* (New York: Henry Holt, 1985). For a powerful personal memoir, see Elie Weisel, *Night* (New York: Bantam, 1982).

25. Sachar, p. 512.
26. Ben Sasson, p. 1021.
27. Sachar, p. 55.
28. Ben Sasson, p. 855.

CHAPTER 6

1. Martin Gilbert, *Israel* (New York: Doubleday, 1998), p. 132.
2. Gilbert, p. 128.
3. Ibid., p. 89.
4. Ibid., p. 148.
5. Minutes of United Nations General Assembly Plenary Meeting, November 26, 1947, found at http://www.zionism-israel.com/zionism_ungromyko2.htm.
6. Gilbert, p. 191.
7. Sachar, pp. 737–39.
8. Deuteronomy 30, Isaiah 55, Jeremiah 31, and Ezekiel 11.
9. Gilbert, pp. 226–28.
10. Quoted in Sachar, p. 762.

CHAPTER 7

1. Israel Bureau of Statistics, 2007.
2. See study of Ben Dror Yemini, April 20, 2007, at www.nrg.co.il/online/ART/564/754.html (Hebrew).
3. Ibid.
4. See Justus Reid Weiner, *Human Rights of Christians in Palestinian Society* (Jerusalem Center for Public Affairs; Jerusalem 2005); David Raab, "The Beleaguered Christians of the Palestinian-Controlled Areas," found at www.jcpa.org//jl/vp490.htm; Khaled Abu Toumeh, "Bethlehem Christians Fear Neighbors," *Jerusalem Post,* January 25, 2007; and Isabel Kershner, "Palestinian Christians Look Back on a Year of Troubles," *New York Times,* March 11, 2007.

5. Khaled Abou Toumeh, "Rapidly Dwindling Christian Minority in Palestinian-Arab-Controlled Areas," *Jerusalem Post,* November 11, 2005.

6. Quotes from *City of Hope* (Jerusalem: Izhak Ben-Zvi Institute, 1996), p. 301.

7. The text of the laws can be found at www.mfa.gov.il/MFA.

8. Greg Myer, *New York Times,* "Trial of Palestinian Leader Focuses Attention on Israeli Courts," May 5, 2003.

9. Israel's Declaration of Independence can be found at www.mfa.gov.il/MFA.

10. Steve Bunstein, *Fascinating Facts about Israel,* Auerbach Central Agency for Jewish Education (Jerusalem, 2006).

CHAPTER 8

1. Bernard Lewis, *The Middle East* (New York: Scribner, 1995), p. 305.

2. Testimony in Peel Commission Report, p.141.

3. Husseini letter to minister for foreign affairs for Hungary, June 28, 1943.

4. Peel Commission Report, pp. 370, 376.

5. Ibid., p. 141.

6. Ian Bickerton and Carla Klausner, *A Concise History of the Arab-Israeli Conflict* (Upper Saddle River, NJ: Prentice Hall, 2002), p. 56.

7. For Israel's request for peace with her neighbors, see the Israeli Declaration of Independence at www.mfa.gov.il/MFA.

8. Sachar, *A History of Israel* (New York: Alfred Knopf, 1976), p. 453.

9. A prominent Palestinian leader, Auni Bey Abdul-Hati, told the Peel Commission, "There is no such country.... Palestine is a term the Zionists invented.... Our country was for centuries part of Syria."

10. Quoted in Gilbert, *Israel,* p. 395.

11. Ibid., p. 394.

12. See Dennis Ross, *The Missing Peace* (Farrar, Straus and Giroux: New York, 2004), and "Don't Play with Maps," *New York Times* op-ed, January 9, 2007.

13. The most comprehensive account of the Oslo and Taba negotiations can be found in Ross, *The Missing Peace.*

14. Ibid.

15. The Palestinian minister of information admitted this was Arafat's policy, stating, "The PA began to prepare for the outbreak of the Intifada since the return from the Camp David negotiations, by request of President Arafat." See Alan Dershowitz, *Why Terrorism Works* (New Haven: Yale University Press 2002), p. 79; and Khaled Abou Toameh, "How the War Began," *Jerusalem Post*, September 20, 2002.

16. For a history of terrorist acts against Israel and Israelis, see www.mfa.gov.il/MFA.

17. David Green, "Fighting by the Book," April 20, 2003.

18. Phyllis Chesler, *The New Anti-Semitism* (Hoboken, NJ: John Wiley, 2003), p. 117.

19. See Alan Dershowitz, *The Case for Israel*, p. 127.

20. *Military Ethics* (Tel Aviv: Ministry of Defense, 1996), Appendix 1, p. 232.

21. Two famous exceptional and indefensible incidents often cited by Arabs are the 1948 massacre in the village of Deir Yassin by members of the Jewish Etzel and Lehi, who were opponents of the official Haganah forces, and the 1994 slaughter of Arabs at prayer in Hebron by Baruch Goldstein. Neither act was ordered by Israeli authorities, and both were violations of Israeli law and condemned by most Israelis.

22. See Dershowitz, *The Case for Israel*, p. 2.

23. April 28, 1948.

24. Sachar, *History of Israel*, p. 382.

25. Haled al Azm, *The Memoirs of Haled al Azm* (Beirut, 1973), part I, pp. 386–87.

26. See Terence Prittie, "Middle East Refugees, in *The Palestinians*, Michael Curtis, ed. (Edison, NJ: Transaction Publishers, 1975), p. 71.

27. Interview with Associated Press, January 1960.

CHAPTER 9

1. See Adam Gregerman, "Old Wine in New Bottles" *Journal of Ecumenical Studies*, vol. 41:2 (2004); and Dexter Van Zile, *Sabeel's Teaching of Contempt: A Judeo-Christian Alliance Report,* June 2005, and *"Sabeel—An Ecumenical Façade to Promote Hatred,* found at www.ngo-monitor.org.

2. "Toward Renovation of the Relationship of Christians and Jews: The Synod of the Protestant Church of the Rheinland, 1908," in *More Stepping Stones to Jewish-Christian Relations,* Helga Croner, ed. (New York: Paulist Press, 1985), pp. 207–209.

3. "Israel, People, Land and State: Aid for Theological Reflection," adopted by the Synod of the Reformed Church of Holland, 1970, in ibid., pp. 99–107.

4. James Parkes, *The End of an Exile: Israel, the Jews and the Gentile World,* Roberta Kalechofsky and Eugene Korn, eds. (Marblehead, MA: Micah Publications, 2005). See also John Pawlikowski, "The Re-Judaization of Christianity—Its Impact on the Church and Its Implications for the Jewish People," Petra Heldt and Malcolm Lowe, Theological Significance of the Rebirth of the State of Israel," and Marcel Dubois, "Jews Judaism and Israel in the Theology of Saint Augustine," all in *People, Land and the State of Israel (Immanuel 22/23)* (Jerusalem: Ecumenical Theological Research Fraternity in Israel, 1989).

5. "What Is the Theological Implication?" *Christian News from Israel* 12:1–2, p. 38.

6. See Bernard Lewis, *Islam and the West* (New York: Oxford University Press, 1993), ch. 2; and *What Went Wrong?* (New York: Oxford University Press, 2002), ch. 4.

7. See "The Cross and the Crescent" in *Catholic World Report,* January 2002; and Charles Sennott, *The Body and the Blood: The Middle East's Vanishing Christians and the Possibility of Peace* (New York, Public Affairs, 2001).

SUGGESTIONS FOR FURTHER READING

Ben Sasson, H. H. *A History of the Jewish People.* Cambridge, MA: Harvard University Press, 1976.

Berkovits, Eliezer. *God, Man and History.* Jerusalem: Shalem Press, 2004.

―――. *Essential Essays on Judaism.* David Hazony, ed. Jerusalem: Shalem Press, 2002.

Dershowitz, Alan. *The Case for Israel.* Hoboken, NJ: John Wiley, 2003.

―――. *The Case for Peace,* Hoboken, NJ: John Wiley and Sons, 2005.

Fisher, Eugene, and Klenicki, Leon. "The Vatican-Israeli Accords: Their Implications for Catholic Faith and Teaching," in *A Challenge Long Delayed.* New York: Anti-Defamation League, 1996.

Facts about Israel. Jerusalem: Israel Information Center. 2006.

Gilbert, Martin. *Atlas of the Arab-Israeli Conflict.* New York: Macmillan, 1974.

―――. *Israel, a History.* New York: William Morrow, 1998.

Hartman, David. *A Living Covenant.* Woodstock, VT: Jewish Lights Publishing, 1998.

Hazony, David. "Eliezer Berkovits, Theologian of Zionism." *Azure* no. 17 (Spring 2004).

Hertzberg, Arthur. *The Zionist Idea*. Philadelphia: Jewish Publication Society, 1959.

Heschel, Abraham Joshua. *Israel: An Echo of Eternity*. Woodstock, VT: Jewish Lights Publishing, 1987.

―――. *End of An Exile: Israel, the Jews and the Gentile World*. Kalechofsky, Roberta, and Eugene Korn, eds. Marblehead, MA: Micah, 2005.

Kenny, Anthony J. *Catholics, Jews and the State of Israel*. New York: Paulist Press, 1993.

Kurzman, Dan. *Genesis 1948*. Cambridge, MA: Da Capo Press, 1992.

Laqueur, Walter. *A History of Zionism*. New York: Schocken Books, 1989.

Lewis, Bernard. *What Went Wrong?* New York: Oxford University Press, 2002.

Lyons, Len. *The Ethiopian Jews of Israel*. Woodstock, VT: Jewish Lights Publishing, 2007.

Parkes, James. *Conflict of the Church and the Synagogue*. New York: Macmillan, 1969.

"People, Land and the State of Israel: Jewish and Christian Perspectives." *Immanuel* 22/23, Jerusalem, 1989.

Ravitsky, Aviezer. *Zionism, Messianism and Jewish Political Radicalism*. Chicago: University of Chicago Press, 1996.

Ross, Dennis. *The Missing Peace*. New York: Farrar, Straus and Giroux, 2004.

Sachar, Howard M. *A History of Israel*. New York: Alfred Knopf, 1976.

Salkin, Jeffry K. *A Dream of Zion: American Jews Reflect on Why Israel Matters to Them.* Woodstock, VT: Jewish Lights Publishing, 2007.

Scheindlin, Raymond. A *Short History of the Jewish People.* New York: Oxford University Press, 2000.

Sennott, Charles. *The Body and the Blood: The Middle East's Vanishing Christians and the Possibility of Peace,* New York: Public Affairs, 2001.

Wilken, Robert. *The Land Called Holy,* New Haven: Yale University Press, 1992.

Current Events/History

A Dream of Zion: American Jews Reflect on Why Israel Matters to Them
Edited by Rabbi Jeffrey K. Salkin Explores what Jewish people in America have to say about Israel. 6 x 9, 304 pp, HC, 978-1-58023-340-8 **$24.99**
Also Available: **A Dream of Zion Teacher's Guide** 8½ x 11, 18 pp, PB, 978-1-58023-356-9 **$8.99**

The Jewish Connection to Israel, the Promised Land: A Brief Introduction for Christians *By Rabbi Eugene Korn, PhD* 5½ x 8½, 176 pp, Quality PB, 978-1-58023-318-7 **$14.99**

The Story of the Jews: A 4,000-Year Adventure—A Graphic History Book
Written & illustrated by Stan Mack 6 x 9, 288 pp, illus., Quality PB, 978-1-58023-155-8 **$16.95**

Hannah Senesh: Her Life and Diary, the First Complete Edition
By Hannah Senesh; Foreword by Marge Piercy; Preface by Eitan Senesh
6 x 9, 368 pp, Quality PB, 978-1-58023-342-2 **$19.99**; 352 pp, HC, 978-1-58023-212-8 **$24.99**

The Ethiopian Jews of Israel: Personal Stories of Life in the Promised Land *By Len Lyons, PhD; Foreword by Alan Dershowitz; Photographs by Ilan Ossendryver*
Recounts, through photographs and words, stories of Ethiopian Jews.
10½ x 10, 240 pp, 100 full-color photos, HC, 978-1-58023-323-1 **$34.99**

Foundations of Sephardic Spirituality: The Inner Life of Jews of the Ottoman Empire
By Rabbi Marc D. Angel, PhD 6 x 9, 224 pp, HC, 978-1-58023-243-2 **$24.99**

Judaism and Justice: The Jewish Passion to Repair the World
By Rabbi Sidney Schwarz 6 x 9, 250 pp, HC, 978-1-58023-312-5 **$24.99**

Ecology/Environment

A Wild Faith: Jewish Ways into Wilderness, Wilderness Ways into Judaism
By Rabbi Mike Comins; Foreword by Nigel Savage
Offers ways to enliven and deepen your spiritual life through wilderness experience.
6 x 9, 240 pp, Quality PB, 978-1-58023-316-3 **$16.99**

Ecology & the Jewish Spirit: Where Nature & the Sacred Meet
Edited by Ellen Bernstein 6 x 9, 288 pp, Quality PB, 978-1-58023-082-7 **$16.95**

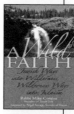

Torah of the Earth: Exploring 4,000 Years of Ecology in Jewish Thought
Vol. 1: Biblical Israel: One Land, One People; Rabbinic Judaism: One People, Many Lands
Vol. 2: Zionism: One Land, Two Peoples; Eco-Judaism: One Earth, Many Peoples
Edited by Arthur Waskow Vol. 1: 6 x 9, 272 pp, Quality PB, 978-1-58023-086-5 **$19.95**
Vol. 2: 6 x 9, 336 pp, Quality PB, 978-1-58023-087-2 **$19.95**

The Way Into Judaism and the Environment
By Jeremy Benstein 6 x 9, 224 pp, HC, 978-1-58023-268-5 **$24.99**

Grief/Healing

Healing and the Jewish Imagination: Spiritual and Practical Perspectives on Judaism and Health *Edited by Rabbi William Cutter, PhD*
Explores Judaism for comfort in times of illness and perspectives on suffering.
6 x 9, 240 pp, HC, 978-1-58023-314-9 **$24.99**

Grief in Our Seasons: A Mourner's Kaddish Companion *By Rabbi Kerry M. Olitzky*
4½ x 6¼, 448 pp, Quality PB, 978-1-879045-55-2 **$15.95**

Healing of Soul, Healing of Body: Spiritual Leaders Unfold the Strength & Solace in Psalms *Edited by Rabbi Simkha Y. Weintraub, CSW*
6 x 9, 128 pp, 2-color illus. text, Quality PB, 978-1-879045-31-6 **$14.99**

Mourning & Mitzvah, 2nd Edition: A Guided Journal for Walking the Mourner's Path through Grief to Healing *By Anne Brener, LCSW*
7½ x 9, 304 pp, Quality PB, 978-1-58023-113-8 **$19.99**

Tears of Sorrow, Seeds of Hope, 2nd Edition: A Jewish Spiritual Companion for Infertility and Pregnancy Loss *By Rabbi Nina Beth Cardin*
6 x 9, 208 pp, Quality PB, 978-1-58023-233-3 **$18.99**

A Time to Mourn, a Time to Comfort, 2nd Edition: A Guide to Jewish Bereavement *By Dr. Ron Wolfson* 7 x 9, 384 pp, Quality PB, 978-1-58023-253-1 **$19.99**

When a Grandparent Dies: A Kid's Own Remembering Workbook for Dealing with Shiva and the Year Beyond *By Nechama Liss-Levinson, PhD*
8 x 10, 48 pp, 2-color text, HC, 978-1-879045-44-6 **$15.95** *For ages 7–13*

Meditation

The Handbook of Jewish Meditation Practices
A Guide for Enriching the Sabbath and Other Days of Your Life
By Rabbi David A. Cooper Easy-to-learn meditation techniques.
6 x 9, 208 pp, Quality PB, 978-1-58023-102-2 **$16.95**

Discovering Jewish Meditation: Instruction & Guidance for Learning an Ancient
Spiritual Practice *By Nan Fink Gefen*
6 x 9, 208 pp, Quality PB, 978-1-58023-067-4 **$16.95**

A Heart of Stillness: A Complete Guide to Learning the Art of Meditation
By David A. Cooper 5½ x 8½, 272 pp, Quality PB, 978-1-893361-03-4 **$16.95** *(A SkyLight Paths book)*

Meditation from the Heart of Judaism: Today's Teachers Share Their Practices,
Techniques, and Faith *Edited by Avram Davis*
6 x 9, 256 pp, Quality PB, 978-1-58023-049-0 **$16.95**

Silence, Simplicity & Solitude: A Complete Guide to Spiritual Retreat at Home
By David A. Cooper 5½ x 8½, 336 pp, Quality PB, 978-1-893361-04-1 **$16.95**
(A SkyLight Paths book)

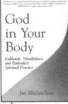

Ritual/Sacred Practice

The Jewish Dream Book: The Key to Opening the Inner Meaning of
Your Dreams *By Vanessa L. Ochs with Elizabeth Ochs; Full-color illus. by Kristina Swarner*
Instructions for how modern people can perform ancient Jewish dream practices
and dream interpretations drawn from the Jewish wisdom tradition.
8 x 8, 128 pp, Full-color illus., Deluxe PB w/flaps, 978-1-58023-132-9 **$16.95**

God in Your Body: Kabbalah, Mindfulness and Embodied Spiritual Practice
By Jay Michaelson
The first comprehensive treatment of the body in Jewish spiritual practice and an
essential guide to the sacred.
6 x 9, 288 pp, Quality PB, 978-1-58023-304-0 **$18.99**

The Book of Jewish Sacred Practices: CLAL's Guide to Everyday & Holiday
Rituals & Blessings *Edited by Rabbi Irwin Kula and Vanessa L. Ochs, PhD*
6 x 9, 368 pp, Quality PB, 978-1-58023-152-7 **$18.95**

Jewish Ritual: A Brief Introduction for Christians
By Rabbi Kerry M. Olitzky and Rabbi Daniel Judson
5½ x 8½, 144 pp, Quality PB, 978-1-58023-210-4 **$14.99**

The Rituals & Practices of a Jewish Life: A Handbook for Personal Spiritual
Renewal *Edited by Rabbi Kerry M. Olitzky and Rabbi Daniel Judson*
6 x 9, 272 pp, illus., Quality PB, 978-1-58023-169-5 **$18.95**

The Sacred Art of Lovingkindness: Preparing to Practice
By Rabbi Rami Shapiro 5½ x 8½, 176 pp, Quality PB, 978-1-59473-151-8 **$16.99**
(A SkyLight Paths book)

Science Fiction/Mystery & Detective Fiction

Mystery Midrash: An Anthology of Jewish Mystery & Detective Fiction
Edited by Lawrence W. Raphael; Preface by Joel Siegel
6 x 9, 304 pp, Quality PB, 978-1-58023-055-1 **$16.95**

Criminal Kabbalah: An Intriguing Anthology of Jewish Mystery & Detective Fiction
Edited by Lawrence W. Raphael; Foreword by Laurie R. King
6 x 9, 256 pp, Quality PB, 978-1-58023-109-1 **$16.95**

Wandering Stars: An Anthology of Jewish Fantasy & Science Fiction
Edited by Jack Dann; Introduction by Isaac Asimov
6 x 9, 272 pp, Quality PB, 978-1-58023-005-6 **$16.95**

More Wandering Stars: An Anthology of Outstanding Stories of Jewish Fantasy and
Science Fiction *Edited by Jack Dann; Introduction by Isaac Asimov*
6 x 9, 192 pp, Quality PB, 978-1-58023-063-6 **$16.95**

Spirituality

Journeys to a Jewish Life: Inspiring Stories from the Spiritual Journeys of American Jews *By Paula Amann*
Examines the soul treks of Jews lost and found. 6 x 9, 208 pp, HC, 978-1-58023-317-0 **$19.99**

The Adventures of Rabbi Harvey: A Graphic Novel of Jewish Wisdom and Wit in the Wild West *By Steve Sheinkin*
Jewish and American folktales combine in this witty and original graphic novel collection. Creatively retold and set on the western frontier of the 1870s.
6 x 9, 144 pp, Full-color illus., Quality PB, 978-1-58023-310-1 **$16.99**
Also Available: **The Adventures of Rabbi Harvey Teacher's Guide**
8½ x 11, 32 pp, PB, 978-1-58023-326-2 **$8.99**

Ethics of the Sages: *Pirke Avot*—Annotated & Explained
Translation and Annotation by Rabbi Rami Shapiro
5½ x 8½, 192 pp, Quality PB, 978-1-59473-207-2 **$16.99** *(A SkyLight Paths book)*

A Book of Life: Embracing Judaism as a Spiritual Practice
By Michael Strassfeld 6 x 9, 528 pp, Quality PB, 978-1-58023-247-0 **$19.99**

Meaning and Mitzvah: Daily Practices for Reclaiming Judaism through Prayer, God, Torah, Hebrew, Mitzvot and Peoplehood *By Rabbi Goldie Milgram*
7 x 9, 336 pp, Quality PB, 978-1-58023-256-2 **$19.99**

The Soul of the Story: Meetings with Remarkable People
By Rabbi David Zeller 6 x 9, 288 pp, HC, 978-1-58023-272-5 **$21.99**

Aleph-Bet Yoga: Embodying the Hebrew Letters for Physical and Spiritual Well-Being
By Steven A. Rapp. Foreword by Tamar Frankiel, PhD and Judy Greenfeld. Preface by Hart Lazer.
7 x 10, 128 pp, b/w photos, Quality PB, Layflat binding, 978-1-58023-162-6 **$16.95**

Does the Soul Survive? A Jewish Journey to Belief in Afterlife, Past Lives & Living with Purpose *By Rabbi Elie Kaplan Spitz; Foreword by Brian L. Weiss, MD*
6 x 9, 288 pp, Quality PB, 978-1-58023-165-7 **$16.99**

First Steps to a New Jewish Spirit: Reb Zalman's Guide to Recapturing the Intimacy & Ecstasy in Your Relationship with God *By Rabbi Zalman M. Schachter-Shalomi with Donald Gropman* 6 x 9, 144 pp, Quality PB, 978-1-58023-182-4 **$16.95**

God in Our Relationships: Spirituality between People from the Teachings of Martin Buber *By Rabbi Dennis S. Ross* 5½ x 8½, 160 pp, Quality PB, 978-1-58023-147-3 **$16.95**

Judaism, Physics and God: Searching for Sacred Metaphors in a Post-Einstein World
By Rabbi David W. Nelson 6 x 9, 368 pp, Quality PB, inc. reader's discussion guide, 978-1-58023-306-4 **$18.99**;
HC, 352 pp, 978-1-58023-252-4 **$24.99**

The Jewish Lights Spirituality Handbook: A Guide to Understanding, Exploring & Living a Spiritual Life *Edited by Stuart M. Matlins*
What exactly is "Jewish" about spirituality? How do I make it a part of my life? Fifty of today's foremost spiritual leaders share their ideas and experience with us.
6 x 9, 456 pp, Quality PB, 978-1-58023-093-3 **$19.99**

Bringing the Psalms to Life: How to Understand and Use the Book of Psalms
By Daniel F. Polish 6 x 9, 208 pp, Quality PB, 978-1-58023-157-2 **$16.95**;
HC, 978-1-58023-077-3 **$21.95**

God & the Big Bang: Discovering Harmony between Science & Spirituality
By Daniel C. Matt 6 x 9, 216 pp, Quality PB, 978-1-879045-89-7 **$16.99**

Minding the Temple of the Soul: Balancing Body, Mind, and Spirit through Traditional Jewish Prayer, Movement, and Meditation *By Tamar Frankiel, PhD, and Judy Greenfeld*
7 x 10, 184 pp, illus., Quality PB, 978-1-879045-64-4 **$16.95**
Audiotape of the Blessings and Meditations: 60 min. **$9.95**
Videotape of the Movements and Meditations: 46 min. **$20.00**

One God Clapping: The Spiritual Path of a Zen Rabbi *By Alan Lew with Sherril Jaffe*
5½ x 8½, 336 pp, Quality PB, 978-1-58023-115-2 **$16.95**

There Is No Messiah ... and You're It: The Stunning Transformation of Judaism's Most Provocative Idea *By Rabbi Robert N. Levine, DD*
6 x 9, 192 pp, Quality PB, 978-1-58023-255-5 **$16.99**

These Are the Words: A Vocabulary of Jewish Spiritual Life
By Arthur Green 6 x 9, 304 pp, Quality PB, 978-1-58023-107-7 **$18.95**

Spirituality/Lawrence Kushner

Filling Words with Light: Hasidic and Mystical Reflections on Jewish Prayer
By Lawrence Kushner and Nehemia Polen
5½ x 8½, 176 pp, Quality PB, 978-1-58023-238-8 **$16.99**; HC, 978-1-58023-216-6 **$21.99**

The Book of Letters: A Mystical Hebrew Alphabet
Popular HC Edition, 6 x 9, 80 pp, 2-color text, 978-1-879045-00-2 **$24.95**
Collector's Limited Edition, 9 x 12, 80 pp, gold foil embossed pages, w/limited edition silkscreened print, 978-1-879045-04-0 **$349.00**

The Book of Miracles: A Young Person's Guide to Jewish Spiritual Awareness
6 x 9, 96 pp, 2-color illus., HC, 978-1-879045-78-1 **$16.95** *For ages 9 and up*

The Book of Words: Talking Spiritual Life, Living Spiritual Talk
6 x 9, 160 pp, Quality PB, 978-1-58023-020-9 **$16.95**

Eyes Remade for Wonder: A Lawrence Kushner Reader *Introduction by Thomas Moore*
6 x 9, 240 pp, Quality PB, 978-1-58023-042-1 **$18.95**

God Was in This Place & I, i Did Not Know: Finding Self, Spirituality and Ultimate Meaning 6 x 9, 192 pp, Quality PB, 978-1-879045-33-0 **$16.95**

Honey from the Rock: An Introduction to Jewish Mysticism
6 x 9, 176 pp, Quality PB, 978-1-58023-073-5 **$16.95**

Invisible Lines of Connection: Sacred Stories of the Ordinary
5½ x 8½, 160 pp, Quality PB, 978-1-879045-98-9 **$15.95**

Jewish Spirituality—A Brief Introduction for Christians
5½ x 8½, 112 pp, Quality PB, 978-1-58023-150-3 **$12.95**

The River of Light: Jewish Mystical Awareness
6 x 9, 192 pp, Quality PB, 978-1-58023-096-4 **$16.95**

The Way Into Jewish Mystical Tradition
6 x 9, 224 pp, Quality PB, 978-1-58023-200-5 **$18.99**; HC, 978-1-58023-029-2 **$21.95**

Spirituality/Prayer

Pray Tell: A Hadassah Guide to Jewish Prayer
By Rabbi Jules Harlow, with contributions from many others
8½ x 11, 400 pp, Quality PB, 978-1-58023-163-3 **$29.95**

Witnesses to the One: The Spiritual History of the *Sh'ma* *By Rabbi Joseph B. Meszler; Foreword by Rabbi Elyse Goldstein* 6 x 9, 176 pp, HC, 978-1-58023-309-5 **$19.99**

My People's Prayer Book Series

Traditional Prayers, Modern Commentaries *Edited by Rabbi Lawrence A. Hoffman*
Provides diverse and exciting commentary to the traditional liturgy, helping modern men and women find new wisdom in Jewish prayer, and bring liturgy into their lives. Each book includes Hebrew text, modern translation, and commentaries from all perspectives of the Jewish world.

Vol. 1—The *Sh'ma* and Its Blessings
7 x 10, 168 pp, HC, 978-1-879045-79-8 **$24.99**
Vol. 2—The *Amidah*
7 x 10, 240 pp, HC, 978-1-879045-80-4 **$24.95**
Vol. 3—*P'sukei D'zimrah* (Morning Psalms)
7 x 10, 240 pp, HC, 978-1-879045-81-1 **$24.95**
Vol. 4—*Seder K'riat Hatorah* (The Torah Service)
7 x 10, 264 pp, HC, 978-1-879045-82-8 **$23.95**
Vol. 5—*Birkhot Hashachar* (Morning Blessings)
7 x 10, 240 pp, HC, 978-1-879045-83-5 **$24.95**
Vol. 6—*Tachanun* and Concluding Prayers
7 x 10, 240 pp, HC, 978-1-879045-84-2 **$24.95**
Vol. 7—Shabbat at Home
7 x 10, 240 pp, HC, 978-1-879045-85-9 **$24.95**
Vol. 8—*Kabbalat Shabbat* (Welcoming Shabbat in the Synagogue)
7 x 10, 240 pp, HC, 978-1-58023-121-3 **$24.99**
Vol. 9—Welcoming the Night: *Minchah* and *Ma'ariv* (Afternoon and Evening Prayer) 7 x 10, 272 pp, HC, 978-1-58023-262-3 **$24.99**
Vol. 10—Shabbat Morning: *Shacharit* and *Musaf* (Morning and Additional Services) 7 x 10, 240 pp, HC, 978-1-58023-240-1 **$24.99**

Theology/Philosophy/The Way Into... Series

The Way Into... series offers an accessible and highly usable "guided tour" of the Jewish faith, people, history and beliefs—in total, an introduction to Judaism that will enable you to understand and interact with the sacred texts of the Jewish tradition. Each volume is written by a leading contemporary scholar and teacher, and explores one key aspect of Judaism. *The Way Into...* series enables all readers to achieve a real sense of Jewish cultural literacy through guided study.

The Way Into Encountering God in Judaism
By Neil Gillman
For everyone who wants to understand how Jews have encountered God throughout history and today.
6 x 9, 240 pp, Quality PB, 978-1-58023-199-2 **$18.99**; HC, 978-1-58023-025-4 **$21.95**
Also Available: **The Jewish Approach to God:** A Brief Introduction for Christians
By Neil Gillman
5½ x 8½, 192 pp, Quality PB, 978-1-58023-190-9 **$16.95**

The Way Into Jewish Mystical Tradition
By Lawrence Kushner
Allows readers to interact directly with the sacred mystical text of the Jewish tradition. An accessible introduction to the concepts of Jewish mysticism, their religious and spiritual significance and how they relate to life today.
6 x 9, 224 pp, Quality PB, 978-1-58023-200-5 **$18.99**; HC, 978-1-58023-029-2 **$21.95**

The Way Into Jewish Prayer
By Lawrence A. Hoffman
Opens the door to 3,000 years of Jewish prayer, making available all anyone needs to feel at home in the Jewish way of communicating with God.
6 x 9, 208 pp, Quality PB, 978-1-58023-201-2 **$18.99**

Also Available: **The Way Into Jewish Prayer Teacher's Guide**
By Rabbi Jennifer Ossakow Goldsmith
8½ x 11, 42 pp, PB, 978-1-58023-345-3 **$8.99**
Visit our website to download a free copy.

The Way Into Judaism and the Environment
By Jeremy Benstein
Explores the ways in which Judaism contributes to contemporary social-environmental issues, the extent to which Judaism is part of the problem and how it can be part of the solution.
6 x 9, 288 pp, HC, 978-1-58023-268-5 **$24.99**

The Way Into Tikkun Olam (Repairing the World)
By Elliot N. Dorff
An accessible introduction to the Jewish concept of the individual's responsibility to care for others and repair the world.
6 x 9, 320 pp, HC, 978-1-58023-269-2 **$24.99**; 304 pp, Quality PB, 978-1-58023-328-6 **$18.99**

The Way Into Torah
By Norman J. Cohen
Helps guide in the exploration of the origins and development of Torah, explains why it should be studied and how to do it.
6 x 9, 176 pp, Quality PB, 978-1-58023-198-5 **$16.99**

The Way Into the Varieties of Jewishness
By Sylvia Barack Fishman, PhD
Explores the religious and historical understanding of what it has meant to be Jewish from ancient times to the present controversy over "Who is a Jew?"
6 x 9, 288 pp, HC, 978-1-58023-030-8 **$24.99**

Theology/Philosophy

I Am Jewish
Personal Reflections Inspired by the Last Words of Daniel Pearl
Almost 150 Jews—both famous and not—from all walks of life, from all around the world, write about many aspects of their Judaism.
Edited by Judea and Ruth Pearl
6 x 9, 304 pp, Deluxe PB w/flaps, 978-1-58023-259-3 **$18.99**
Download a free copy of the *I Am Jewish Teacher's Guide* **at our website:**
www.jewishlights.com

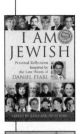

A Touch of the Sacred: A Theologian's Informal Guide to Jewish Belief
By Dr. Eugene B. Borowitz and Frances W. Schwartz Explores the musings from the leading theologian of liberal Judaism. 6 x 9, 256 pp, HC, 978-1-58023-337-8 **$21.99**

Talking about God: Exploring the Meaning of Religious Life with Kierkegaard, Buber, Tillich and Heschel *By Daniel F. Polish, PhD*
Examines the meaning of the human religious experience with the greatest theologians of modern times. 6 x 9, 160 pp, HC, 978-1-59473-230-0 **$21.99** *(A SkyLight Paths book)*

Jews & Judaism in the 21st Century: Human Responsibility, the Presence of God, and the Future of the Covenant
Edited by Rabbi Edward Feinstein; Foreword by Paula E. Hyman
Five celebrated leaders in Judaism examine contemporary Jewish life.
6 x 9, 192 pp, HC, 978-1-58023-315-6 **$24.99**

The Death of Death: Resurrection and Immortality in Jewish Thought
By Neil Gillman 6 x 9, 336 pp, Quality PB, 978-1-58023-081-0 **$18.95**

Ethics of the Sages: Pirke Avot—Annotated & Explained
Translation & Annotation by Rabbi Rami Shapiro
5½ x 8½, 208 pp, Quality PB, 978-1-59473-207-2 **$16.99** *(A SkyLight Paths book)*

Hasidic Tales: Annotated & Explained
By Rabbi Rami Shapiro; Foreword by Andrew Harvey
5½ x 8½, 240 pp, Quality PB, 978-1-893361-86-7 **$16.95** *(A SkyLight Paths Book)*

A Heart of Many Rooms: Celebrating the Many Voices within Judaism
By David Hartman 6 x 9, 352 pp, Quality PB, 978-1-58023-156-5 **$19.95**

The Hebrew Prophets: Selections Annotated & Explained
Translation & Annotation by Rabbi Rami Shapiro; Foreword by Zalman M. Schachter-Shalomi
5½ x 8½, 224 pp, Quality PB, 978-1-59473-037-5 **$16.99** *(A SkyLight Paths book)*

Keeping Faith with the Psalms: Deepen Your Relationship with God Using the Book of Psalms *By Daniel F. Polish* 6 x 9, 320 pp, Quality PB, 978-1-58023-300-2 **$18.99**

A Living Covenant: The Innovative Spirit in Traditional Judaism
By David Hartman 6 x 9, 368 pp, Quality PB, 978-1-58023-011-7 **$20.00**

Love and Terror in the God Encounter
The Theological Legacy of Rabbi Joseph B. Soloveitchik
By David Hartman 6 x 9, 240 pp, Quality PB, 978-1-58023-176-3 **$19.95**

The Personhood of God: Biblical Theology, Human Faith and the Divine Image
By Dr. Yochanan Muffs; Foreword by Dr. David Hartman 6 x 9, 240 pp, HC, 978-1-58023-265-4 **$24.99**

Traces of God: Seeing God in Torah, History and Everyday Life
By Neil Gillman 6 x 9, 240 pp, HC, 978-1-58023-249-4 **$21.99**

Your Word Is Fire: The Hasidic Masters on Contemplative Prayer
Edited and translated by Arthur Green and Barry W. Holtz
6 x 9, 160 pp, Quality PB, 978-1-879045-25-5 **$15.95**

Travel

Israel—A Spiritual Travel Guide, 2nd Edition
A Companion for the Modern Jewish Pilgrim
By Rabbi Lawrence A. Hoffman 4¾ x 10, 256 pp, Quality PB, illus., 978-1-58023-261-6 **$18.99**
Also Available: **The Israel Mission Leader's Guide** 978-1-58023-085-8 **$4.95**

Judaism / Christianity

Christians and Jews in Dialogue: Learning in the Presence of the Other
by Mary C. Boys and Sara S. Lee; Foreword by Dorothy C. Bass
Inspires renewed commitment to dialogue between religious traditions and illuminates how it should happen. Explains the transformative work of creating environments for Jews and Christians to study together and enter the dynamism of the other's religious tradition.
6 x 9, 240 pp, HC, 978-1-59473-144-0 **$21.99**

Healing the Jewish-Christian Rift: Growing Beyond Our Wounded History
by Ron Miller and Laura Bernstein; Foreword by Dr. Beatrice Bruteau
6 x 9, 288 pp, Quality PB, 978-1-59473-139-6 **$18.99**

Introducing My Faith and My Community
The Jewish Outreach Institute Guide for the Christian in a Jewish Interfaith Relationship
by Rabbi Kerry M. Olitzky 6 x 9, 176 pp, Quality PB, 978-1-58023-192-3 **$16.99** *(a Jewish Lights book)*

The Jewish Approach to God: A Brief Introduction for Christians
by Rabbi Neil Gillman 5½ x 8½, 192 pp, Quality PB, 978-1-58023-190-9 **$16.95** *(a Jewish Lights book)*

Jewish Holidays: A Brief Introduction for Christians
by Rabbi Kerry M. Olitzky and Rabbi Daniel Judson
5½ x 8½, 176 pp, Quality PB, 978-1-58023-302-6 **$16.99** *(a Jewish Lights book)*

Jewish Ritual: A Brief Introduction for Christians
by Rabbi Kerry M. Olitzky and Rabbi Daniel Judson
5½ x 8½, 144 pp, Quality PB, 978-1-58023-210-4 **$14.99** *(a Jewish Lights book)*

Jewish Spirituality: A Brief Introduction for Christians
by Rabbi Lawrence Kushner
5½ x 8½, 112 pp, Quality PB, 978-1-58023-150-3 **$12.95** *(a Jewish Lights book)*

A Jewish Understanding of the New Testament
by Rabbi Samuel Sandmel; new Preface by Rabbi David Sandmel
5½ x 8½, 368 pp, Quality PB, 978-1-59473-048-1 **$19.99**

We Jews and Jesus
Exploring Theological Differences for Mutual Understanding
by Rabbi Samuel Sandmel; new Preface by Rabbi David Sandmel A Classic Reprint
Written in a non-technical way for the layperson, this candid and forthright look at the what and why of the Jewish attitude toward Jesus is a clear and forceful exposition that guides both Christians and Jews in relevant discussion.
6 x 9, 192 pp, Quality PB, 978-1-59473-208-9 **$16.99**

Kabbalah / Mysticism / Enneagram

Awakening to Kabbalah: The Guiding Light of Spiritual Fulfillment
by Rav Michael Laitman, PhD 6 x 9, 192 pp, HC, 978-1-58023-264-7 **$21.99**

Cast in God's Image: Discover Your Personality Type Using the Enneagram and Kabbalah
by Rabbi Howard A. Addison 7 x 9, 176 pp, Quality PB, 978-1-58023-124-4 **$16.95**

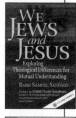

Ehyeh: A Kabbalah for Tomorrow *by Dr. Arthur Green*
6 x 9, 224 pp, Quality PB, 978-1-58023-213-5 **$16.99**

The Enneagram and Kabbalah, 2nd Edition: Reading Your Soul
by Rabbi Howard A. Addison 6 x 9, 192 pp, Quality PB, 978-1-58023-229-6 **$16.99**

Finding Joy: A Practical Spiritual Guide to Happiness *by Dannel I. Schwartz with Mark Hass*
6 x 9, 192 pp, Quality PB, 978-1-58023-009-4 **$14.95**

The Gift of Kabbalah: Discovering the Secrets of Heaven, Renewing Your Life on Earth
by Tamar Frankiel, PhD 6 x 9, 256 pp, Quality PB, 978-1-58023-141-1 **$16.95**
HC, 978-1-58023-108-4 **$21.95**

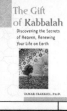

Honey from the Rock: An Easy Introduction to Jewish Mysticism
by Lawrence Kushner 6 x 9, 176 pp, Quality PB, 978-1-58023-073-5 **$16.95**

Kabbalah: A Brief Introduction for Christians
by Tamar Frankiel, PhD 5½ x 8½, 176 pp, Quality PB, 978-1-58023-303-3 **$16.99**

Zohar: Annotated & Explained *Translation and Annotation by Dr. Daniel C. Matt*
Foreword by Andrew Harvey 5½ x 8½, 176 pp, Quality PB, 978-1-893361-51-5 **$15.99**

About Jewish Lights

People of all faiths and backgrounds yearn for books that attract, engage, educate, and spiritually inspire.

Our principal goal is to stimulate thought and help all people learn about who the Jewish People are, where they come from, and what the future can be made to hold. While people of our diverse Jewish heritage are the primary audience, our books speak to people in the Christian world as well and will broaden their understanding of Judaism and the roots of their own faith.

We bring to you authors who are at the forefront of spiritual thought and experience. While each has something different to say, they all say it in a voice that you can hear.

Our books are designed to welcome you and then to engage, stimulate, and inspire. We judge our success not only by whether or not our books are beautiful and commercially successful, but by whether or not they make a difference in your life.

For your information and convenience, at the back of this book we have provided a list of other Jewish Lights books you might find interesting and useful. They cover all the categories of your life:

Bar/Bat Mitzvah	Life Cycle
Bible Study / Midrash	Meditation
Children's Books	Parenting
Congregation Resources	Prayer
Current Events / History	Ritual / Sacred Practice
Ecology/ Environment	Spirituality
Fiction: Mystery, Science Fiction	Theology / Philosophy
Grief / Healing	Travel
Holidays / Holy Days	12-Step
Inspiration	Women's Interest
Kabbalah / Mysticism / Enneagram	

Stuart M. Matlins, Publisher

Or phone, fax, mail or e-mail to: **JEWISH LIGHTS Publishing**
Sunset Farm Offices, Route 4 • P.O. Box 237 • Woodstock, Vermont 05091
Tel: (802) 457-4000 • Fax: (802) 457-4004 • www.jewishlights.com
Credit card orders: **(800) 962-4544** (8:30AM–5:30PM ET Monday–Friday)
Generous discounts on quantity orders. SATISFACTION GUARANTEED. Prices subject to change.